THE PEOPLE'S CHOICE COOKBOOK

CONTENTS

Thank you for buying this book. You have helped to further the work of the League of Women Voters of Minnesota to promote political responsibility through an informed citizenry.

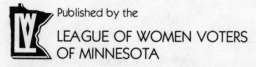 Published by the

LEAGUE OF WOMEN VOTERS
OF MINNESOTA

555 Wabasha, St. Paul, Minnesota 55102
612/224-5445

Printed by Bolger Publications/Creative Printing Inc., Minneapolis
©Copyright 1983 League of Women Voters of Minnesota
International Standard Book Number 0-939816-04-0

INTRODUCTION

Well known for the high caliber of its research and service in the public interest, the League of Women Voters of Minnesota has long been a significant factor in the good life to be found in Minnesota. For over sixty years, the League has worked to assure the preservation of our clean environment, excellent schools, vibrant cities and responsive government.

In the development of THE PEOPLE'S CHOICE COOKBOOK, we discovered that the League reputation for excellence extends to the kitchen as well. Often we were able to draw upon members' professional skills as home economists, editors, artists, and marketers. But most of all we relied upon the creativity and culinary traditions of League members and friends from hundreds of communities throughout the state who contributed their choice recipes to this book.

THE PEOPLE'S CHOICE COOKBOOK is a uniquely Minnesota grassroots product. We hope through this book we can share with you our enthusiasm for good food and the good life, Minnesota-style.

The Cookbook Committee

Joann Buie, chair

standing committee

Virginia Allen	Connie Hondl
Diana Barsness	Margaret Leppik
Patricia Buysman	Marcia Walters
Judy Cipolla	Jane McKinlay, *artist*
Georgeann Hall	Betsy Norum, *consultant*

ad hoc committee

Jeanne Crampton	Jennifer Leslie
Laurie Culbert	Nadeen Mutsch
Elizabeth Ebbott	Meredith Poland
Zelma Gray	Kathleen Stiegler
Barbara Hendershott	Doris Van Campen
Rose Isenhart	

APPETIZERS & BEVERAGES ☑

Raw Vegetable Dip
"make ahead for flavors to blend"

1 cup mayonnaise
½ cup dairy sour cream
2 teaspoons chives
¼ teaspoon paprika

⅛ teaspoon curry powder
½ teaspoon Worcestershire sauce
1 tablespoon grated onion
1 clove garlic, crushed

Mix all ingredients and refrigerate 12-24 hours. Serve with raw vegetables. This dip keeps for several weeks in the refrigerator.

Yield: 1½ cups.

Debate Dip
"score points"

3 tablespoons grated onion
3 tablespoons catsup
3 tablespoons honey
1 tablespoon curry powder

½ teaspoon chili powder
2 cups mayonnaise
1 tablespoon lemon juice

Mix all ingredients together and refrigerate overnight. Serve with raw vegetables such as broccoli, cauliflower, mushrooms and zucchini.

Yield: about 2 cups.

Soap-Box Spinach Dip
"share with a crowd"

1 cup dairy sour cream
1 cup mayonnaise
1 (10 oz.) package frozen
   chopped spinach, thawed
   and completely drained

1 (8 oz.) can water chestnuts,
   drained and chopped
1 (1⅝ oz.) package Knorr dry
   vegetable soupmix
1 large loaf unsliced Jewish rye
   or party rye bread

Combine all ingredients except bread. Refrigerate dip for at least 2 hours before serving.

Hollow out center of bread to within 1 inch of edge. Cut bread from center into bite-size pieces. Just before serving, place spinach dip in hollowed-out bread, surround with cut-up pieces for dipping.

Yield: about 4 cups.

Variation: 1 (8 oz.) package softened cream cheese may be substituted for ½ cup of the sour cream.

Fresh Minted Topping or Dip

"for fresh fruit"

1 cup vanilla yogurt
1 tablespoon finely chopped
    fresh mint

2 tablespoons frozen orange juice
    concentrate, thawed
1 tablespoon honey

Combine all ingredients; stir until blended. Cover and refrigerate. Serve as a dip or spoon over fresh fruit.

Yield: 1¼ cups.

Avocado-Yogurt Dip

"milder than guacamole"

1 cup plain yogurt
1 large ripe avocado, peeled,
    seeded and coarsely chopped
2 shallots, chopped
1 green onion, chopped

½ teaspoon dried tarragon
⅛ teaspoon oregano
1 teaspoon lemon juice
⅛ teaspoon salt
¼ teaspoon pepper

Combine all ingredients in blender and mix until smooth; refrigerate. Serve as fresh vegetable dip or as dressing on a fresh vegetable salad.

Yield: about 1½ cups.

Hot Pecan Dip

"for the rank and file"

1 (8 oz.) package cream cheese,
    softened
1 (3 oz.) package cream cheese,
    softened
3 tablespoons milk
4 oz. dried beef, chopped

½ cup chopped green pepper
1 small onion, chopped
¼ teaspoon garlic salt
⅛ teaspoon pepper
½ cup dairy sour cream
⅔ cup pecan halves

Combine cream cheese, milk, dried beef, green pepper, onion, garlic salt and pepper; fold in sour cream. Spread in 8-inch pie pan or ovenproof dish. Arrange pecans on top. Bake at 350 degrees for 20 minutes. Serve hot with crackers.

Yield: 20 servings.

Hot Artichoke Dip

"can easily be cut in half"

2 (14 oz.) cans artichoke hearts,
   drained and finely chopped
1 cup mayonnaise

1 cup plain yogurt
1 teaspoon garlic salt
2 cups grated Parmesan cheese

Combine all ingredients; spread in 10-inch pie pan. Bake at 350 degrees for 30 minutes. Serve hot with crackers.

Yield: 30-40 servings.

Chili Dip

"make a double batch — it goes fast"

1 (14½ oz.) can stewed tomatoes,
   thoroughly drained
1 (8 oz.) package cream cheese,
   softened

1 (4 oz.) can chopped green
   chilies, drained

Combine all ingredients in mixer or blender. Refrigerate several hours. Serve with taco chips.

Yield: 2 cups.

Curried Almond-Stuffed Olives

"zippy"

¾ cup toasted slivered almonds,
   finely chopped
¼ teaspoon dried tarragon
½ teaspoon paprika
1 teaspoon curry powder
¼ teaspoon pepper

Salt (optional)
2 teaspoons dried parsley
4 oz. cream cheese
2 tablespoons cream
2 (7 oz.) cans pitted green
   or ripe olives

Mix together all ingredients except olives. Slice olives in half, fill with cheese mixture and put halves back together. Refrigerate.

Yield: 50 olives.

Guacamole in Cherry Tomatoes

"Prepare in the summer when cherry tomatoes are at their best."

12 medium to large cherry
tomatoes
1 ripe avocado, peeled and
seeded
1 small clove garlic, minced

1 tablespoon minced onion
1 tablespoon chopped green chili
peppers or green chili Taco
sauce to taste
2 teaspoons fresh lemon juice
Fresh parsley, washed and dried

Cut thin slice off top of each tomato; scoop out seeds with small spoon; invert on paper towels to drain.

Mash avocado; combine with garlic, onion, chilies and lemon juice. Fill tomatoes with guacamole. Sprinkle a little lemon juice on top of guacamole to prevent it from turning brown. Top with a parsley sprig and refrigerate.

Yield: 1 dozen.

Caviar Mousse

"before taxes"

4 oz. red lumpfish caviar
3 tablespoons chopped fresh
parsley
2 tablespoons finely minced onion
¼ teaspoon freshly ground
pepper

1 cup dairy sour cream
1½ teaspoons unflavored gelatin
2 tablespoons water
½ cup whipping cream, whipped
Cucumber slices
Rye melba toast

Set aside 2 tablespoons caviar, 1 tablespoon parsley and 1 tablespoon onion for garnish; cover and refrigerate.

Combine remaining caviar, parsley and onion with pepper and sour cream in medium-size non-metal bowl and blend well.

Sprinkle gelatin over water in small saucepan. Stir over low heat until gelatin dissolves. Remove from heat and stir into caviar mixture.

Fold in whipped cream. Turn into 2-cup non-metal bowl or mold or crock. Cover and refrigerate until set.

Let stand at room temperature 15 minutes. Unmold (or spoon from crock) onto non-metal plate. Surround with cucumber slices and rye melba toast. Garnish top with reserved caviar, onion and parsley.

Pretty with red impatients blossoms, including a few leaves.

Yield: 8-12 servings.

Chicken Artichoke Mousse
"many flavors subtly blended"

1 envelope unflavored gelatin
1 cup water
½ cup dairy sour cream or yogurt
1 (3 oz.) package cream cheese, softened
¼ cup mayonnaise
¼ cup dry white wine
1 teaspoon dried marjoram, crushed
1 teaspoon dry mustard
¼ teaspoon salt
¼ teaspoon freshly ground black pepper
1 medium chicken breast, cooked, boned and skin removed
1 (14 oz.) can artichoke hearts, drained
2 hard-cooked eggs
2 green onions
1 cup shredded carrot

In heat-proof measuring cup, combine gelatin and water. Place cup in a saucepan of hot water. Heat and stir until gelatin is dissolved. Transfer to mixing bowl. Beat in sour cream, cream cheese, mayonnaise, wine, marjoram, dry mustard, salt and pepper.

Grind chicken, artichokes, eggs and green onions through fine blade of food grinder or chop finely in food processor. Add carrot; mix well.

Fold into gelatin mixture. Spoon into 4½-cup mold (or two 2-cup molds). Refrigerate until firm. Unmold and serve with vegetable dippers.

Yield: 4 cups.

Reception Liver Pâté
"a crunchy version of this buffet table favorite"

2 envelopes unflavored gelatin
½ cup cold water
2¼ cups consommé madrilène, heated
1 (3½ oz.) package slivered almonds
1 (7½ oz.) can ripe olives, drained and sliced
1 pound canned liver pâté

Soften gelatin in cold water. Mix gelatin and consommé together. Put one quarter of mixture in glass loaf pan and chill slightly. Decoratively arrange half of almonds and olives in chilled consommé mixture.

Chop remaining olives. Add with remaining almonds and liver pâté to remaining consommé and carefully pour over chilled consommé in pan. Refrigerate several hours until firm.

Unmold and serve with assorted crackers.

Yield: 35-40 servings at a reception.

Baked Mushroom Caps
"first call is all that's necessary"

12 very large mushrooms
3 tablespoons margarine
1 small onion, chopped
1 cup soft bread crumbs
½ cup diced cooked ham
2 oz. (½ cup) shredded Cheddar cheese

⅛ teaspoon marjoram, rosemary or oregano
2 tablespoons cream or sherry
2 tablespoons grated Parmesan cheese
¼ cup broth or water

Wash mushrooms and remove stems; chop stems. In large skillet, melt 2 tablespoons margarine and sauté mushroom caps on all sides. Remove mushrooms and juice from skillet.

Sauté chopped stems and chopped onion in 1 tablespoon margarine. Remove from heat. Add bread crumbs, ham, cheese, seasoning and cream. Cook 2 minutes.

Fill mushroom caps and sprinkle with Parmesan cheese. Put mushrooms in baking pan with skillet juice and broth. Bake at 350 degrees for 20 minutes. Broil about 6 inches from heat for about 2 minutes.

Yield: 12 appetizers or 4 first course servings.

Variation: Use chicken, shrimp, cooked bacon or ¼ cup unsalted nuts in place of the ham.

Mugwump Mushrooms
"for the indecisive hostess"

1 pound medium-size fresh mushrooms, stems removed

4 ounces Boursin, Rondele or other spiced-herb cheese
Fresh parsley, washed and dried

Wipe mushrooms clean with damp paper towel. Stuff with generous amount of cheese. Top with a parsley sprig; refrigerate.

Yield: about 3 dozen.

Pecans Worcestershire
"a party favorite"

2 cups large pecan halves
⅓ cup Worcestershire sauce
1 tablespoon butter

2 dashes Tabasco sauce
Salt (optional)

Mix all ingredients together on warm cookie sheet. Bake at 300 degrees for 15-20 minutes or until crisp. Stir several times during baking.

Yield: 2 cups.

Cheese Ball
"popular party spread"

1 (8 oz.) package cream cheese or neufchatel cheese, softened
8 oz. (2 cups) shredded sharp Cheddar cheese
2 tablespoons mayonnaise
1 tablespoon lemon juice

1 tablespoon minced green pepper
¾ teaspoon onion powder or 1 small onion, chopped
Chopped nuts or finely snipped parsley

Mix all ingredients except nuts together until well blended. Form into a ball; roll in nuts. Top with a maraschino cherry if desired. Chill until serving.

Yield: 6-8 servings.

Blue Cheese Balls
"make ahead of time"

2 (8 oz.) packages cream cheese, softened
4 oz. crumbled blue cheese
1 (5 oz.) jar Old English cheese spread

Dash of Worcestershire sauce
½ teaspoon onion powder
Chopped almonds or minced parsley

Combine cheeses with electric mixer or by hand. Add Worcestershire sauce and onion powder and mix again. Refrigerate mixture for about 1 hour for easier handling.

Divide mixture in 3 parts. Shape into balls and roll each in chopped nuts or parsley. Wrap each ball separately in plastic wrap and refrigerate until serving. Serve with crackers.

Balls can be frozen and used later.

Yield: 3 cheese balls.

Salmon Spread
"wins a vote of confidence"

1 (15½ oz.) can red salmon,
drained
1 (8 oz.) package cream cheese,
softened
1 tablespoon minced onion

⅛ teaspoon freshly ground
pepper
3 tablespoons mayonnaise
1 teaspoon Worcestershire sauce
Fresh parsley

Remove large bones and dark skin from salmon. Gently mix all ingredients except parsley with a fork. Place in a crock and refrigerate at least 4 hours.

Top with parsley. Serve with pita bread pieces, crackers or raw vegetables.

Yield: 3 cups.

Cheese Spritz
"a crisp, cheesy wafer"

1¼ cups (5 oz.) shredded sharp
Cheddar cheese
¼ cup margarine, softened
⅔ cup flour

¼ teaspoon salt
1 tablespoon grated Parmesan
cheese

Heat oven to 350 degrees. Using mixer or food processor, mix all ingredients together to form a dough. Put dough through cookie press onto ungreased cookie sheet. Bake for 20 minutes or until edges of wafers just begin to brown.

Yield: 2 dozen.

Grecian Meatballs
"cinnamon distinguishes these"

2 pounds lean ground beef
1 cup fine bread crumbs
1 cup finely chopped onion
½ cup water
1 egg

1 tablespoon salt
1 teaspoon pepper
½ teaspoon cinnamon
1 teaspoon garlic powder
2½ teaspoons oregano

Blend all ingredients together. Form into 1-inch balls. Place meatballs in jelly roll pan or in 13x9x2-inch pan. Bake at 350 degrees for 35 minutes or until done.

Meatballs can be made in advance and served cold or reheated and served hot in a chafing dish.

Yield: 100 cocktail-size meatballs.

Cheese and Spinach Puffs

"a hearty appetizer"

4 eggs, slightly beaten
2 cups herb stuffing mix
2 (10 oz.) packages frozen
    chopped spinach, thawed
    and drained
1 cup finely chopped onion

⅓ cup margarine or butter,
    melted
½ cup grated Parmesan cheese
1 cup (4 oz.) shredded sharp
    Cheddar cheese
½ teaspoon garlic salt
1 teaspoon thyme

Combine all ingredients; mix thoroughly. Refrigerate for 1 hour. Shape mixture into balls the size of a walnut. Place on jelly roll pan; cover with aluminum foil. Refrigerate at least 30 minutes before baking.

Heat oven to 350 degrees. Bake for 10-12 minutes. Serve warm.

Yield: 5 dozen.

Shrimp Cocktail Eggs

"When I brought these to a church social, the platter never made it to the table!"

12 hard-cooked eggs
⅓ cup mayonnaise
¼ cup cocktail sauce
2 teaspoons lemon juice

¼ teaspoon salt
1 (4.25 oz.) can small or medium
    shrimp, drained
Chives or parsley

Shell eggs; halve and remove yolks to a bowl. Mash yolks; add mayonnaise, cocktail sauce, lemon juice and salt. Blend until smooth.

Fill whites with mixture. Place one or two shrimp, depending on size, on top of each egg half; garnish with chives or parsley.

Yield: 24 halves.

Senator's Shrimp Dip

"gets a standing ovation"

2 (4½ oz.) cans shrimp
1 (8 oz.) package cream cheese,
    softened
½ cup butter, melted

½ cup mayonnaise
2 tablespoons lemon juice
Dash of Worcestershire sauce
1-2 tablespoons grated onion

Blend ingredients together and refrigerate overnight. Serve on crackers.

Dip will keep for long periods of time when refrigerated.

Yield: 3 cups.

Parmesan Knots
"with a different twist this could be a loophole"

3 (7.5 oz.) cans refrigerated
buttermilk biscuits
½ cup oil
½ cup grated Parmesan cheese

2 teaspoons garlic powder
1 tablespoon oregano
¼ teaspoon pepper
1 tablespoon dried parsley flakes

Cut each biscuit into thirds. Roll and stretch each piece and tie in a knot. Bake as directed on biscuit package.

Mix remaining ingredients together. Pour over baked knots. Stir continually until they have absorbed as much of the seasoning mixture as possible.

To serve, reheat at 350 degrees for 5-7 minutes.

To freeze knots, pour the unabsorbed seasoning mixture over the knots and freeze together. Defrost and reheat to serve.

Yield: 70 knots.

Pickled Eggs
"This is one of the 7 sweets and 7 sours that all supper tables had on them in the German-speaking sections of Pennsylvania."

10-12 small round fresh beets
or 1 (8¼ oz.) can small
whole beets
½ cup vinegar
2 tablespoons sugar

½ teaspoon salt
¼ teaspoon cloves
1 bay leaf
1 small onion, thinly sliced
6 hard-cooked eggs

If using fresh beets, clean well, put in saucepan, cover with water and cook until tender. Remove beets; slide off the skins. Add vinegar, sugar, salt, cloves, bay leaf and onion to beet juice. Bring to a boil.

Shell eggs. Place in container with beets and juice. Make sure beet juice covers eggs and beets. Refrigerate overnight or until eggs turn a bright pink.

Remove eggs from marinade, slice in half and serve on an egg dish with some of the pickled beets.

Refrigerate beet juice; it can be used several times to color more hard-cooked eggs.

Yield: 12 servings.

Wontons

"Wontons are the favorites in my cooking classes for children."

2-3 green onions
2 large stalks celery
Few spinach greens or Chinese
  cabbage leaves
1 (8 oz.) can bamboo shoots
1 (8 oz.) can water chestnuts
3 large mushrooms
½ cup bean sprouts

12 Chinese pea pods
6 medium shrimp, cooked
1 tablespoon soy sauce
1 tablespoon sherry
1 package wonton wrappers
1 egg white, beaten with
  a little water
Peanut oil for frying
Sweet Sour Sauce (below)

Finely chop vegetables and shrimp. Toss together with soy sauce and sherry. Refrigerate 1 hour or more.

Place teaspoon of mixture in center of wonton wrapper and fold bottom corner of wonton skin over filling to opposite corner, forming a triangle. Brush right corner of triangle with egg white. Bring corners together below filling; pinch left corner to right corner to seal. Repeat with remaining wonton skins.

Keep wrappers and prepared wontons covered with plastic wrap to prevent drying out. Heat peanut oil in wok or heavy skillet.

Fry a few wontons at a time until golden. Drain on paper towels. Keep warm in 150 degree oven. Serve with hot mustard or Sweet Sour Sauce.

To freeze, cool and place in plastic bags. Reheat at 350 degrees for about 15 minutes or until crisp.

Yield: about 50 wontons.

Sweet Sour Sauce:

1 (6 oz.) can unsweetened
  pineapple juice
¼ cup cider vinegar
1 tablespoon soy sauce
2 tablespoons sugar
½ cup beef broth

¼ cup shredded sweet red
  pepper (optional)
2 teaspoons finely chopped
  fresh ginger
2 tablespoons cornstarch
⅓ cup water

Combine all ingredients except cornstarch and water in medium saucepan; bring to boil.

Mix cornstarch and water in small cup; add to boiling sauce, stirring constantly. Continue to cook, stirring, until sauce is thickened and clear, about 1 minute.

Sauce will keep covered in refrigerator up to 1 week.

Yield: about 2 cups.

Hamburger Sausage
"delicious with cheese and crackers"

5 pounds ground beef
2½ teaspoons mustard seed
2½ teaspoons ground pepper
2½ teaspoons garlic salt

5-6 teaspoons liquid smoke
2 tablespoons plus 2 teaspoons curing salt
1 teaspoon Spice Islands Old Hickory smoked salt

Combine all ingredients in large bowl; knead mixture. Cover and refrigerate.

Knead mixture once daily for 4 days. On the 5th day, form into 5 sausage rolls (use waxed paper). Place rolls on a jelly roll pan.

Bake at 200 degrees for about 4 hours. After about 2 hours, pour fat from pan and continue baking until all fat is rendered off.

Sausage freezes well.

Yield: Five 1-pound rolls.

Warek Eenab
(Stuffed Grape Leaves)
"Middle East folklore credits the grape leaf as the food of the blessed."

1 jar grape leaves, drained
1 cup uncooked rice
1 pound extra-lean ground beef
2 tablespoons butter, melted
¼ teaspoon cinnamon

1 teaspoon salt
⅛ teaspoon pepper
2 teaspoons crumbled dried mint leaves
¼ cup lemon juice

Line bottom of Dutch oven or large heavy kettle with a layer of grape leaves.

Mix rice, ground beef, butter and spices together. With backside of grape leaf facing up, place one tablespoonful of meat mixture on one end of leaf; fold over three sides and roll toward the fourth side to form a neat roll.

Layer rolls evenly on leaves in pan. Add enough water to cover ¼ inch over rolls. Use an inverted plate to keep rolls immersed. Cover pan and cook rolls over low heat until rice is cooked, about 20-30 minutes. Add lemon juice and simmer an additional 5 minutes.

Serve hot as an appetizer, accompaniment or entrée.

Yield: 8-10 appetizer servings; 6 entrée servings.

Strawberry Punch

"bright red punch with the taste of fresh strawberries"

1 (10 oz.) package frozen
strawberries, partially thawed
1 quart ginger ale, chilled

3 (6 oz.) cans frozen lemonade
concentrate, thawed
3 (6 oz.) cans water

Whirl strawberries in blender. Add lemonade and water; whirl again. Pour into punch bowl and add ginger ale.

Yield: 18-20 (4 oz.) servings.

Summer Planter's Punch

"a sweet refresher for a hot summer day"

2 quarts cold tea
1 (6 oz.) can frozen lemonade
concentrate, thawed

⅓ cup grenadine syrup
2 teaspoons almond extract

Combine all ingredients; chill and serve.

Yield: 18 (4 oz.) servings.

Cold Quack

"lame duck diet punch"

1 quart black cherry-flavored
diet soda
1 quart strawberry-flavored
diet soda

2 quarts grapefruit-flavored
diet soda
¼ cup red wine vinegar
Lemon and orange slices

Pour all sodas and vinegar into punch bowl containing ice. Float lemon and orange slices.

Yield: 24 (4 oz.) servings.

Rose Garden Punch

"a beautiful punch for a wedding or special occasion"

1 (6 oz.) can frozen lemonade
  concentrate, thawed
1 (6 oz.) can frozen orange juice
  concentrate, thawed

1 quart ginger ale, chilled
1 pint white catawba grape juice,
  chilled
2 juice cans water (optional)

Combine all ingredients in punch bowl or large pitcher. If desired, float a "wedding ring" of flowers frozen in ice.

Yield: 18-20 (4 oz.) servings.

Cranberry Punch

"colorful for the holidays"

1 (6 oz.) can frozen orange juice
  concentrate, thawed
1 (6 oz.) can frozen pink lemonade
  concentrate, thawed
1 (6 oz.) can frozen pineapple
  juice concentrate, thawed

5 cups cold water
6 cups cranberry juice cocktail
3½ cups (28 oz.) ginger ale,
  chilled

Mix all ingredients except ginger ale. Pour over ice. Add ginger ale. Float orange and lime slices, if desired.

Yield: 32 (4 oz.) servings.

Mulled Cider

"for a cold day after skating"

½ gallon apple cider
1 quart cranapple or cranberry
  juice cocktail
1 (6 oz.) can frozen pineapple
  juice concentrate

1 (6 oz.) can water
3 cinnamon sticks
2 tablespoons whole cloves
¼ teaspoon allspice

Place juices and water in 4-quart kettle. Tie spices in cheese cloth bag; place in kettle and simmer 15 minutes. If using 30-cup electric coffee pot, place spices in coffee basket and perk cider through spices.

Yield: 27 (4 oz.) servings.

Prohibition Wassail

"Carrie Nation wouldn't approve, but 1 cup bourbon can be added."

1 teaspoon whole cloves
1 teaspoon whole allspice
3-inch cinnamon stick
Dash nutmeg
2 quarts apple cider

1 teaspoon brandy flavoring
1 teaspoon rum flavoring
Orange slices
Brown sugar (optional)

Put spices in a tea ball or tie in cheese cloth. Combine remaining ingredients in 4-quart crockery cooker and heat on high for 1 hour or heat just to boiling in large saucepan and simmer for 20 minutes.

Remove spices and turn cooker to low. Add orange slices and brown sugar to taste.

For an unusual presentation, stick whole cloves in oranges and bake at 325 degrees for 30 minutes in a pan with a little water. Substitute for orange slices.

Yield: 16-18 (4 oz.) servings.

Cider Punch

"a viable alternative"

1 gallon apple cider
2 (6 oz.) cans frozen orange juice
   concentrate

1 (6 oz.) can frozen lemonade
   concentrate
½ teaspoon ginger
½ teaspoon cinnamon

Heat all ingredients together in large, old-fashioned enamel coffee pot or 30-cup electric pot.

Yield: 36 (4 oz.) servings.

Frozen Daiquiri Punch

"A double batch just fits in a 5-quart ice cream bucket."

3 (6 oz.) cans frozen lemonade
concentrate, thawed
3 (6 oz.) cans frozen limeade
concentrate, thawed

18 oz. (3 juice cans) white rum
1 quart 7-up
Filbert nuts

Place ingredients, except filberts, in a plastic container with a tight-fitting cover. Mix well and cover. Place in freezer until frozen. (Time can vary from 4-12 hours, depending on freezer.)

Before serving, stir until the consistency of slush. Serve in 6-ounce glasses using a filbert for a garnish.

Unused punch will keep well if refrozen.

Yield: 15 (6 oz.) servings.

Brandy Slush

"a quantity recipe for a nice summer cooler"

7 cups cold tea
2 cups brandy
1 (12 oz.) can frozen orange juice
concentrate, thawed

1 (12 oz.) can frozen lemonade
concentrate, thawed
1½ cups sugar
1 quart 7-up or club soda

Mix all ingredients except 7-up and freeze in a 5-quart ice cream bucket. When ready to serve, put ¾ cup slush mixture and ¼ cup 7-up for each serving desired in a blender. Blend a few seconds until smooth.

Yield: 16 (8 oz.) servings.

Lady Slipper Punch

"sparkling summer drink"

2 pints fresh strawberries
1-2 cups powdered sugar
1 bottle white Moselle wine

2 bottles Champagne, chilled
½ bottle claret, chilled

Wash, hull and halve strawberries. Sprinkle with powdered sugar. Pour ½ bottle Moselle over strawberries. Chill 2-6 hours. When ready to serve, add rest of Moselle, chilled Champagne and claret. If this is too strong, 1 quart ginger ale may be added.

Yield: 22 (4 oz.) servings.

Hot Tomato Bouillon

"an easy, light soup served in cups for a crowd"

6 quarts tomato juice
6 quarts water
20 beef bouillon cubes

2 cups sugar (or less to taste)
3 (2-inch) cinnamon sticks
1 tablespoon whole cloves

Mix all ingredients in a large kettle. Heat to boiling; lower heat and simmer 1 hour. Remove cinnamon sticks and cloves before serving. Serve hot.

Yield: 96 (4 oz.) servings.

Hot or Cold Spiced Tea

"an all-weather drink"

2 quarts water
5 tablespoons instant tea
1 (16 oz.) can pineapple juice
1 (12 oz.) can frozen orange juice
   concentrate, reconstituted

1 (12 oz.) can frozen lemonade
   concentrate, reconstituted
2-3 cups sugar (to taste)
4 cinnamon sticks
2 tablespoons whole cloves
2 cups boiling water

In large container, mix 2 quarts water and instant tea. Add pineapple juice, orange juice, lemonade and sugar.

Steep cinnamon sticks and cloves in boiling water in teapot for 5 minutes. Strain; add to tea and juice mixture.

Heat all ingredients together to serve hot or refrigerate to serve cold.

Yield: 26 (8 oz.) servings.

SOUPS ☑

Broccoli Soup
"served after a hot tub party"

3 tablespoons butter
2 tablespoons flour
2 cups milk
¼ teaspoon white pepper
2 cups chicken broth
2 tablespoons chicken bouillon
   granules
3 carrots, finely chopped

5 (5½ oz.) cans chunk chicken or
   2½ cups diced cooked
   chicken
2 pounds fresh broccoli, finely
   chopped
1 medium onion, chopped
½ pound fresh mushrooms,
   chopped

Melt butter in 4-quart kettle. Add flour; stir and pour in milk. Add remaining ingredients except mushrooms. Cook over low heat 1 hour. Add mushrooms; cook 3 minutes more. Looks nice served with a raw broccoli floweret atop each serving.

Yield: 4 quarts.

Green Bean Soup
"delicious served with whole grain bread and cheese"

1½ pounds fresh green beans,
   cut into 1-inch slices
2 cups diced potatoes
2 cups sliced onion
¼ teaspoon ground pepper
1 teaspoon thyme
3 bay leaves

2 leaves fresh sage
   or pinch of dried sage
½ teaspoon salt
1¾ quarts water
1 pint dairy sour cream
   or plain yogurt

In 4-quart kettle put beans, potatoes, onions, pepper, thyme, bay leaves, sage, salt and water. Bring to a boil, turn down to simmer and cook uncovered until vegetables are tender, about 30 minutes.

Remove sage leaves and refrigerate 24 hours to allow flavors to blend. While soup is still cold, stir in sour cream. Reheat to serving temperature. Do not boil.

Yield: 10 (8 oz.) servings.

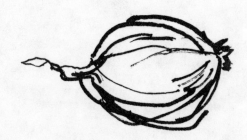

French Onion Soup au Gratin
"a French-Canadian recipe"

4 medium onions, thinly sliced
4 tablespoons butter
2 (10½ oz.) cans beef broth
2 broth cans water
1 teaspoon Worcestershire sauce
4 drops Tabasco sauce
3 tablespoons red wine

Few peppercorns
1 clove garlic
1 bay leaf
4-6 slices toasted French bread or
  Holland rusk
1 cup (4 oz.) shredded mozzarella
  or Gruyère cheese

In large kettle, sauté onions in butter until transparent. Add broth, water, Worcestershire sauce, Tabasco sauce and wine. Tie spices in cheesecloth bag; add to soup. Cover and simmer 2 hours.

At serving time, remove spices. Place a slice of toasted bread in each bowl. Pour soup over bread. Divide cheese evenly between bowls of soup. Broil until cheese melts and is bubbly and brown.

Yield: 4-6 servings.

Fresh Onion Mushroom Soup
"Your friends will lobby for this recipe."

2 tablespoons butter
3 medium onions, coarsely
  chopped
1 pound fresh mushrooms, sliced
1 quart hot chicken bouillon
⅓ cup minced fresh parsley
3 tablespoons tomato paste
1 clove garlic, crushed
¼ teaspoon freshly ground
  pepper

½ cup dry white wine
1 cup (4 oz.) shredded Jarlsberg
  cheese
1 cup (4 oz.) shredded Cheddar
  cheese
1 cup (4 oz.) grated Parmesan
  cheese
4-6 slices caraway cocktail rye
  bread, quartered and toasted

Melt butter in Dutch oven over medium-high heat. Add onions and sauté until almost tender. Add mushrooms and sauté. Stir in bouillon, parsley, tomato paste, garlic and pepper. Increase heat and quickly bring soup to a boil. Reduce heat and add wine. Cover and simmer 5 minutes.

Combine cheeses; divide toast and cheese among 4 (6 oz.) soup bowls or mugs. Ladle hot soup over cheese and serve immediately.

Yield: 4 main course or 8 first course servings.

Pea Soup Plus

"cook in a crockpot while serving as an election judge"

2 Polish (or other type) sausages
1 large onion, cut up
2 tablespoons chopped green
  pepper
1 tablespoon butter
¾ cup dry split peas, washed
1 quart water
1 clove garlic, crushed

2-3 sprays of celery leaves
1 teaspoon chicken stock base
  or 2 chicken bouillon cubes
1 small potato, cut up
2 carrots, sliced
1 stalk celery, sliced
Salt

Cut sausages into small pieces and brown lightly. Sauté onion and green pepper in butter. In large kettle, place sausage, onion, green pepper, split peas, water, garlic, celery leaves and chicken stock base. Cover and simmer for about 2½-3 hours or until peas are tender.

Add potato, carrots and celery. Simmer 30 minutes longer or until vegetables are tender but still firm. Salt to taste.

Yield: 4-6 servings.

Anoka Pumpkin Soup

"a delicious end for a Halloween jack-o-lantern"

1 onion, sliced
6 green onions, chopped
¼ cup butter
3½ pounds fresh pumpkin
  (about 8 cups), peeled and
  cut in 1-inch chunks
1½ quarts chicken broth

½ teaspoon salt
3 tablespoons flour
3 tablespoons butter
1 cup light cream
1 cup whipping cream
Pinch of salt

In large kettle, sauté onions in ¼ cup butter until soft. Add pumpkin, broth and ½ teaspoon salt. Bring to a boil; reduce heat and simmer 15 minutes or until pumpkin is soft. Whirl in blender until smooth; return to kettle.

Blend flour and 3 tablespoons butter with fork. Gradually add to soup while beating with whisk. Bring to a boil, whisking until thick. Turn heat down; add light cream.

Just before serving, whip whipping cream and pinch of salt until stiff. Serve soup topped with a dollop of whipped cream.

Yield: 8-12 servings.

Variation: 3 cups canned pumpkin may be substituted for fresh pumpkin. The pumpkin flavor will be stronger.

Potato Soup Munich
"an import that enhances international relations"

4 slices thick-sliced lean bacon, diced
6 leeks, sliced (white portion and 1 inch of green)
1 medium onion, diced
2-3 tablespoons flour
1 quart beef broth

3 potatoes, thinly sliced
2 egg yolks
1 cup dairy sour cream
2 tablespoons chopped fresh parsley
1 tablespoon chervil

In soup pot, sauté bacon 5-7 minutes until browned. Add leeks and onion; sauté 5 minutes.

Drain off all but 2-3 tablespoons of fat. Stir in flour; slowly stir in beef broth. Add potatoes and simmer, covered, 1 hour.

Beat egg yolks and combine with sour cream. Stir into soup and heat through. Do not boil. Stir in parsley and chervil before serving.

Can be made ahead and reheated before adding sour cream.

Yield: 6 servings.

Gazpacho
"cool, crisp and refreshing"

1 (28 oz.) can whole tomatoes
1 large green pepper, cut up
5 stalks celery, diced
½ cup cider vinegar
6 green onions including tops, cut up
1 large unpeeled cucumber, cut up

1 (46 oz.) can tomato juice
3 tablespoons olive oil
3 tablespoons Worcestershire sauce
½-1 tablespoon Tabasco sauce
Freshly ground pepper, to taste

Whirl vegetables together in batches in blender. Transfer to gallon container. Add tomato juice, oil and seasonings; refrigerate 24 hours. Stir well before serving.

Keeps well in covered container in refrigerator up to one month.

Yield: 24 (6 oz.) servings.

Squash Bisque
"delicious in fall served with hot popovers"

3 tablespoons butter
1 cup minced onion
¼ cup minced carrot
Salt and pepper to taste
2 medium potatoes, peeled
  and cubed
1 quart chicken broth

2 acorn squash, peeled and
  cubed, about 3-3½ cups
½ cup whipping cream
½ cup milk
½ teaspoon salt
¼ teaspoon pepper
Dash cayenne pepper (optional)

Melt butter in 1½-quart saucepan. Add onion and carrot and sprinkle lightly with salt and pepper. Cook, covered, 10 minutes or until vegetables are tender.

Add potatoes, chicken broth and squash. Simmer, covered, over low heat about 25 minutes until vegetables are very tender. Force mixture through sieve or fine disk of food mill or blend in blender.

Return puréed mixture to saucepan and add whipping cream and milk. Cook soup until heated through; add ½ teaspoon salt and ¼ teaspoon pepper. Pour soup into tureen and serve in cups, sprinkling each with cayenne pepper.

Yield: 8 servings.

Variation: 2 (10 oz.) packages frozen squash may be used in place of acorn squash.

Tomato-Potato Soup
"cross-country skiing and then soup"

3 onions, sliced
1 large carrot, thinly sliced
½ cup margarine
4 cups canned Italian tomatoes
Pinch of sugar
1 teaspoon salt

Freshly ground pepper
2 large potatoes, peeled and
  sliced
3 tablespoons tomato paste
½ teaspoon baking soda
1 cup whipping cream

Sauté onions and carrot in margarine. Drain tomatoes; reserve liquid and add water to make 4 cups. Add tomatoes, liquid, sugar, salt, pepper, potatoes and tomato paste. Simmer 1 hour, partially covered.

Put through food mill or food processor. Add baking soda and cream; heat to serving temperature.

Yield: 10-12 servings.

Variation: Substitute milk for whipping cream for a lighter soup.

Tomato Consommé
"an attractive light soup — perfect for a first course"

1 (10¾ oz.) can chicken broth 1¼ cups tomato juice
1 (10½ oz.) can consommé Thin lemon slices

Heat broth, consommé and tomato juice together. Serve with a lemon slice on top.

Yield: 4-6 servings.

Vegetable Barley Soup
"makes an excellent 'peasant meal' when served with whole grain bread, cheese and fresh fruit"

¾ cup diced onion 4 vegetable bouillon cubes
1 cup diced celery with leaves ⅓ cup barley
1 cup diced carrots 1 bay leaf
⅓ cup vegetable oil 2 whole cloves
4 cups cubed eggplant 3 sprigs fresh parsley
2½ cups diced zucchini 1 (16 oz.) can tomatoes
1½ cups chopped cauliflower 1½ teaspoons salt
1 cup diced unpeeled potato 1 teaspoon ground oregano
1 cup cut green beans ½ teaspoon pepper
6 cups water

In large kettle, sauté onion, celery and carrots in oil 5 minutes or until onion is transparent. Add eggplant, zucchini, cauliflower, potato and green beans. Stir over moderate heat 10 minutes.

Add water, bouillon cubes and barley; stir occasionally to dissolve the bouillon cubes. Tie bay leaf, cloves and parsley in cheesecloth or put in tea ball to form bouquet garni. Add with remaining ingredients.

Cover and simmer 45 minutes or until barley is cooked and vegetables are just tender. Discard bouquet garni.

Yield: 8 servings.

Vegetable Chowder
"wonderfully thick and chunky"

3 cups sliced fresh mushrooms
3 leeks, sliced
1 (10 oz.) package frozen cut
asparagus, thawed and
drained
6 tablespoons butter or margarine
3 tablespoons flour
½ teaspoon salt

½ teaspoon pepper
2 (10¾ oz.) cans chicken broth
2 cups half and half cream
1 (12 oz.) can white whole kernel
corn
1 tablespoon chopped pimiento
Dash of saffron, crushed in
a little water

Sauté mushrooms, leeks and asparagus in butter until tender but not brown. Stir in flour, salt and pepper. Add chicken broth and cream. Cook and stir until mixture is thick. Stir in corn, pimiento and saffron. Heat thoroughly but do not boil.

Can be frozen and reheated in double boiler.

Yield: 6-8 servings.

Variation: Substitute milk for cream for a lighter soup.

Zucchini Soup
"well seasoned"

1 medium clove garlic, minced
1 medium onion, chopped
3 medium zucchini (about 2½
pounds), cut up
2 (7½ oz.) cans chicken broth
1 cup water

1 teaspoon salt
⅛ teaspoon pepper
¼ cup chopped fresh parsley
1½ teaspoons oregano
Seasoned salt to taste

Put all ingredients in saucepan. Bring to a boil, reduce heat and simmer 30 minutes. Purée in blender. Serve warm.

Quantity is easily adjusted. Freezes well.

Yield: 10-12 servings.

Hot or Cold Zucchini Soup
"a negotiable soup"

1 cup chopped onion	2 teaspoons salt
1 cup chopped green pepper	¼ teaspoon black pepper
3 tablespoons butter	3 tablespoons chopped fresh
6 cups zucchini chunks	parsley
1 large clove garlic, minced	¼ teaspoon tarragon

Sauté onion and green pepper in butter until soft. Add zucchini, garlic, salt and black pepper. Cook 10-15 minutes in tightly covered pan, stirring once. Stir in parsley and tarragon.

Put in blender and process until smooth. Serve hot or cold.

Peel and remove seeds if using large zucchini.

Yield: 1½ quarts.

Wild Rice Soup
"elegant enough for a formal dinner"

⅔ cup uncooked wild rice	⅓ cup shredded carrot
2 tablespoons butter	⅓ cup diced celery
1 tablespoon minced onion	⅓ cup sliced fresh mushrooms
¼ cup flour	1 cup half and half cream
1 quart chicken broth	2 tablespoons sherry
½ teaspoon salt	Fresh parsley

Rinse wild rice, soak in cold water 1 hour; drain. Cover with boiling water and cook over low heat 40 minutes.

Melt butter in 4-quart pan and sauté onion. Blend in flour. Gradually add broth and cook, stirring constantly, until slightly thickened.

Stir in rice, salt, carrot, celery and mushrooms. Simmer 5 minutes. Add cream and sherry. Heat to serve. Garnish with parsley.

Yield: 6 bowls or 12 cups.

Norwegian Meatball Soup

"Prepared over 2 days — my grandmother served this soup as a first course on Christmas Eve with lefse and cheeses."

2-3-pound beef soup bone with meat
1½-2-pound veal soup bone with meat
4 quarts cold water
Assorted cut-up raw vegetables, such as carrots, celery, and cabbage

2 medium Spanish onions
2 teaspoons salt
3 peppercorns
1 bay leaf
3 quarts cold water
Norwegian Meatballs (below)

Place all ingredients except 3 quarts cold water and meatballs in large kettle. Bring to a boil; reduce heat and simmer until vegetables are tender.

Remove vegetables. Continue to simmer until meat falls off bones, about 4-6 hours; add water as necessary. Remove meat and bones; strain broth.

Cover bones again with 3 quarts cold water; bring to a boil. Simmer for another hour. Add water as needed. Remove bones and strain. Combine first and second extractions of broth; cover and chill overnight. Skim off fat.

Heat broth to simmering; drop meatballs into broth. Simmer 15 minutes.

Taste improves when soup is chilled again overnight. Heat to serve.

Yield: 1½ gallons; 24 (1 cup) servings.

Norwegian Meatballs:

5 pounds beef round steak, ground 5 times*
1-2 cups whipping cream

Minced onion to taste
1 teaspoon ginger
Salt and pepper to taste

Mix all ingredients thoroughly and knead until of uniform consistency. Form meatballs the size of large walnuts.

*Ask your butcher to grind the meat. The results will be a very fine-grained meatball.

Yield: 12 dozen.

Muriel's Beef Soup

"This is a hearty old family recipe my father used to make. It was Hubert's favorite and now is Max's too. Hubert liked to tell everyone it gave him vigor and vitality."

1½ pounds beef stew meat or chuck
1 beef soup bone
1 quart cold water
1 teaspoon salt
1 teaspoon pepper
2 bay leaves
4-5 medium carrots, sliced (about 2 cups)
½ cup chopped onion

1 cup chopped celery
1 cup chopped cabbage
1 (20 oz.) can Italian style tomatoes, chopped (2½ cups)
1 tablespoon Worcestershire sauce
1 beef bouillon cube
⅛ teaspoon oregano, thyme, celery seed and/or your preferred spices

Cover meat and soup bone with cold water in heavy 3-quart kettle. Add salt, pepper and bay leaves. Bring to a boil; skim off foam for a clearer soup. Reduce heat, cover and simmer for at least 2½ hours or until meat is tender.

When tender, remove bone and bay leaves. If the meat is in one big piece, cut into bite-size pieces. Add vegetables, Worcestershire sauce, bouillon cube and spices. Simmer again until vegetables are tender, about 30 minutes.

"Serve with fruit salad, a glass of milk, lots of crackers and dessert. Soup is low in calories but high in food value."

Yield: 6-8 servings.

Saturday Session Soup

"serve other days too"

2 pounds lean prime beef, cubed
2 tablespoons butter
2 cups cubed onion
2 cups cubed carrots
½ cup chopped celery tops
1 cup chopped cabbage
2 cups peeled, cubed potatoes
2 quarts hot water

1½ teaspoons salt
½ teaspoon freshly ground pepper
2 bay leaves
¼ teaspoon sweet basil
¾ teaspoon beef flavor base or beef bouillon granules
1½ cups tomato juice

Brown meat in butter; add onion and cook 5 minutes. Add rest of ingredients except tomato juice; bring to a boil. Cover; reduce heat and simmer 20 minutes. Add tomato juice; simmer 10 minutes more.

Yield: 10-12 servings.

Simplest Bouillabaisse

"A hearty bread and green salad are perfect complements."

1 cup chopped onion
1-2 cloves garlic, chopped
2 tablespoons olive oil
2 cups dry vermouth or
  dry white wine
2 cups marinara or spaghetti
  sauce

2 (8 oz.) bottles clam juice
Salt and pepper to taste
1½-2 pounds firm white fish
  (torsk, orange ruffie, cod)
Lemon juice
Chopped fresh parsley or
  green onion

In large saucepan, sauté onion and garlic in olive oil until onion is limp but not brown. Add vermouth, marinara sauce and clam juice; simmer. Season with salt and pepper.

Cut fish into 3-inch chunks. Drizzle with lemon juice. Add fish to simmering broth. (Broth should cover fish; if it doesn't, add a little water.) Cover pan; simmer 7-15 minutes depending on size of fish pieces. Fish is done when it is opaque and flakes when tested with a fork. Serve with garnish of chopped parsley or green onion.

Yield: 4 servings.

Caraway Shrimp Soup

"a soup or an entrée"

8 oz. fresh mushroom caps,
  chopped (about 2 cups)
3 tablespoons butter
⅛ teaspoon freshly ground
  pepper
½ teaspoon salt
1 teaspoon garlic powder
½ cup flour

3 (10¾ oz.) cans chicken broth
1 (10 oz.) can clams and juice
1 pound shrimp, cooked and
  cleaned
1 teaspoon caraway seed
1½ teaspoons dill weed
1 cup whipping cream

Sauté mushrooms in butter. Add pepper, salt, garlic powder and flour; stir well. Add broth, stirring constantly. Bring to a boil.

Add clams and juice, shrimp, caraway seed and dill; simmer 15-30 minutes.

Add whipping cream just before serving. Heat through.

Yield: 8 servings.

Variation: To serve as an entrée over rice, reduce chicken broth to 1 can and whipping cream to ⅓ cup.

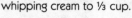

Artichoke Shrimp Soup
"good with Swiss Cheese Bread"

1 (10¾ oz.) can condensed cream of mushroom soup
1 (10¾ oz.) can condensed cream of celery soup
1 cup chicken broth or 1 chicken bouillon cube in 1 cup boiling water
⅛ teaspoon curry powder
1 (14 oz.) can artichoke hearts, drained and cut in quarters
1 (4½ oz.) can or 1 (8 oz.) bag cocktail shrimp, cooked and cleaned
1 (8 oz.) can sliced water chestnuts

Mix all ingredients in 2-quart saucepan and heat thoroughly.

Yield: 4 (8 oz.) servings.

Cold Shrimp Soup
"a cool soup for a hot Minnesota day"

1 quart stewed tomatoes, cut in bite-size pieces
1 cup tomato juice
⅓ cup diced green pepper
½ cup diced celery
½ cup diced onion
1 (3½ oz.) can tiny shrimp
2 tablespoons sugar
2 teaspoons salt
1 tablespoon horseradish
¼ cup vinegar

Mix all ingredients; chill and serve with crackers on the side.

Yield: 8-12 servings.

Treasure Cave Blue Soup
"good reason to come in out of the cold"

1 head cabbage, chopped
½ cup butter or margarine
1 medium head cauliflower, coarsely chopped
7 cups chicken broth
1 cup whipping cream
¼ cup (1 oz.) blue cheese
Salt and freshly ground pepper to taste
Croutons

In 4-quart saucepan, cook cabbage in butter until transparent, stirring occasionally. Add cauliflower and chicken broth; simmer 30 minutes.

Blend cream and cheese thoroughly. Stir into soup. Season with salt and pepper. Garnish with croutons.

Yield: 10 servings.

Cheese Soup

"great way to use up old cheeses"

1 cup chopped celery
1 cup chopped carrots
1 cup chopped potatoes
1 quart chicken broth
½ cup finely chopped onion

¼ cup butter or margarine
⅓ cup flour
1 quart milk
1½-2 cups (6-8 oz.) shredded
   Cheddar cheese

In 4-quart cooking pot, simmer vegetables in chicken broth until tender.

In 2-quart saucepan, cook onion in butter until tender, but not brown. Blend in flour; gradually add milk. Cook and stir over medium-high heat until thick. Remove from heat. Add cheese and stir until melted.

Remove broth from heat and stir in cheese mixture.

Yield: 3½ quarts.

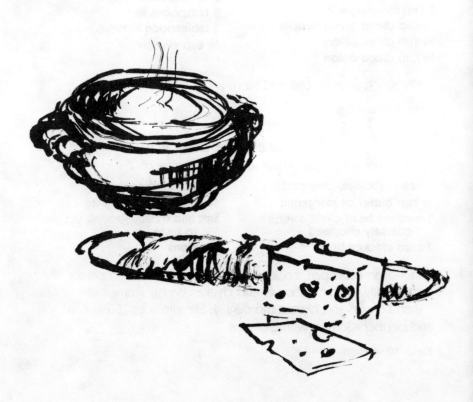

BREADS ☑

Note about measuring flour: When measuring flour, there is no need to sift before measuring. Lightly spoon flour into measuring cup and level with straight edge of a spatula or knife. When flour is mixed with other dry ingredients, just stir to blend.

The World's Best Bread
"multilateral support"

2 packages active dry yeast
½ cup warm water
   (105-115 degrees)
1 teaspoon granulated sugar
About 6 cups unbleached flour
1½ cups warm water
2 cups whole wheat flour
1½ cups rye flour
½ cup soy flour

½ cup rolled oats
½ cup corn meal
½ cup packed brown sugar
½ cup vegetable oil
2 tablespoons salt
3 tablespoons molasses
3 tablespoons wheat germ
1 tablespoon brewer's yeast

Dissolve yeast in ½ cup water; add granulated sugar. Mix enough unbleached flour with 1½ cups warm water to make thin batter. Combine yeast mixture and flour mixture. Stir until smooth; cover and set in warm place to rise, about 45 minutes.

Add remaining ingredients, including 3-4 cups unbleached flour to make stiff dough. Oil hands and knead 15 minutes on lightly floured surface. Cover; let rise in warm place until double in bulk, about 1 hour.

Punch down; let rise again. Shape into 4 loaves; place in greased 8x4x2½-inch loaf pans and let rise.

Heat oven to 350 degrees. Bake for 50 minutes.

Yield: 4 loaves.

Swiss Cheese Bread
"party perfect"

1 (1 pound) loaf French bread
8 oz. Swiss cheese, thinly sliced
1 cup margarine, melted

1 large onion, finely minced
2 tablespoons poppy seed

Cut French bread into 1½-inch slices, not quite through loaf. Place 1 slice of cheese in each cut. Mix margarine with onion and poppy seed. Spoon mixture between slices.

Wrap in foil and heat at 350 degrees for 15-20 minutes.

Yield: 8-10 servings.

French Bread

"a state fair winner"

2½ cups warm water
  (105-115 degrees)
2 packages active dry yeast
1 tablespoon salt
1 tablespoon margarine, melted

7 cups all-purpose flour
Cornmeal or flour
1 egg
1 tablespoon cold water

Measure warm water into large mixing bowl. Add yeast, stir to dissolve. Add salt and margarine. Add flour and stir until well blended (dough will be sticky). Turn out on lightly floured surface and knead until smooth. Place in greased bowl, turn to grease top. Cover and let rise in warm palce until doubled in bulk, about 1 hour.

Turn dough onto lightly floured surface. Divide into 2 equal portions. Roll each into a 15x10-inch oblong. Beginning at wide end, roll up, seal edges and taper ends. Place loaves seam side down on greased cookie sheets sprinkled with cornmeal. Cover; let rise in warm place until doubled.

Heat oven to 450 degrees. Make 4 diagonal cuts on top of each loaf. Bake for 25 minutes. Remove from oven, brush with egg mixed with cold water. Return to oven and bake 5 minutes longer.

Yield: 2 loaves.

Variations: Substitute whole wheat for half the all-purpose flour. Dough can be shaped in rounds or bread sticks. For bread sticks, shape in pencil-size sticks, brush with egg mixture before baking and sprinkle with coarse salt, poppy seed, etc. Bake at 450 degrees for about 15 minutes.

Raisin Batter Bread

"a quick no-knead yeast bread"

1 package active dry yeast
½ cup warm water
   (105-115 degrees)
1 teaspoon cinnamon
¼ teaspoon ground ginger
3 tablespoons sugar

1 (13 oz.) can evaporated milk
1 teaspoon salt
2 tablespoons vegetable oil
3½-4 cups all-purpose flour
½ cup raisins

In large bowl, dissolve yeast in water; blend in spices and 1 tablespoon sugar. Let stand in warm place until bubbly (about 15 minutes). Stir in remaining sugar, milk, salt and oil. Gradually beat in flour to make heavy, stiff and sticky batter. Mix in raisins.

Spoon batter into well-greased 2-pound coffee can or two 1-pound cans. Cover with greased plastic can lids. Batter may be frozen at this point and thawed later for baking.

Let batter rise in warm place until plastic lids pop off, about 50-60 minutes.

Heat oven to 350 degrees. Bake 2-pound can for about 1 hour, 1-pound cans for about 45 minutes.

Let bread cool in can on wire rack for 10 minutes, then loosen around edge with thin knife and remove from can. Allow to cool in upright position on rack.

Yield: 1 large or 2 small loaves.

Honey Graham Bread

"Great for meat sandwiches, especially when toasted."

2 packages active dry yeast
½ cup warm water
   (105-115 degrees)
2 teaspoons sugar
1¾ cups lukewarm milk
½ cup honey
1 tablespoon salt

3 tablespoons dried onion
   (optional)
¼ cup shortening
3¾ cups stone-ground
   graham flour
2½ cups all-purpose flour

Dissolve yeast in water; add sugar. Combine milk, honey and salt in large mixing bowl; stir. Add onion. Beat in shortening, yeast mixture and 1 cup graham flour with beater until smooth. Add remaining flour gradually. Mix until dough leaves side of bowl.

Turn onto lightly floured surface. Knead until smooth and elastic, at least 10 minutes. Place in lightly greased bowl; cover and let rise in warm place until double in bulk, about 1-1½ hours. Punch down and let rise again until nearly double, 45-60 minutes.

Divide in half and shape into loaves. Place in greased 9x5x3-inch pans. Cover and let rise for 1 hour.

Heat oven to 375 degrees. Bake for 40-45 minutes.

Yield: 2 loaves.

Whole Wheat Bread

"This bread is very heavy and makes great toast. If used without toasting, it should be cut very thin."

2 packages active dry yeast
¾ cup warm water
   (105-115 degrees)
2⅔ cups warm skim milk
5 tablespoons margarine
2 tablespoons sugar
1 tablespoon molasses
1½ tablespoons salt

4 cups whole wheat or
   graham flour
1 cup rolled oats
½ cup wheat germ
¾ cup walnuts, finely chopped
1 tablespoon caraway seed
   (optional)
4 cups stone-ground white flour

Dissolve yeast in water. Add milk, margarine, sugar, molasses and salt. Add 3 cups whole wheat flour and beat with beater. Add one cup whole wheat flour and beat by hand 150 strokes. Add rolled oats, wheat germ, walnuts and caraway seed; beat well. Add white flour, beat and turn onto floured surface.

Knead 15 minutes or until dough is smooth and no longer sticks to surface (it may take additional flour). Place in bowl; cover with plastic wrap and dish towel and let rise in warm place about 20 minutes, or until double in bulk.

Cut dough in half; with palm of hand, flatten each half into rectangle and roll into loaf. Put in well-oiled 9x5x3-inch loaf pan; cover lightly with waxed paper and refrigerate. Let rise at least 2 but not more than 24 hours.

Heat oven to 400 degrees. Bake for 50 minutes. Turn out of pans immediately and cool on wire rack.

Yield: 2 loaves.

Swedish Limpa
"from the north country"

2 cups water
¼ cup packed brown sugar
¼ cup honey
1½ teaspoons caraway seed
1 tablespoon lard

2 packages active dry yeast
4 cups all-purpose flour
2 cups rye flour
1 teaspoon salt
Melted shortening

Heat water, brown sugar, honey, caraway seed and lard; cool to lukewarm (105-115 degrees). Add yeast. Mix well and add about 3 cups all-purpose flour. Beat thoroughly. Add rye flour, salt and additional all-purpose flour to make a dough that can be easily handled.

Turn onto lightly floured surface and knead until smooth and elastic. Place dough in greased bowl. Let rise in warm place until double, 2-4 hours.

Knead and shape into 2 round loaves. Place in greased 9-inch pie pans. Brush tops with melted shortening and let rise again 1-2 hours.

Heat oven to 350 degrees. Bake for about 60 minutes.

Yield: 2 round loaves.

Poppy Seed Bread
"A very easy recipe — especially good for a beginning bread baker who wants something a little different."

2 packages active dry yeast
2½ cups warm water
   (105-115 degrees)
¼ cup margarine, softened
¼ cup poppy seed
¼ cup sugar

1 tablespoon salt
6-7 cups all-purpose flour
1 egg white
1 tablespoon cold water
1 tablespoon poppy seed

In large bowl, dissolve yeast in water. Add margarine, ¼ cup poppy seed, sugar and salt. Stir in 2-3 cups flour. Beat until well blended. Stir in enough additional flour to make a soft dough. Cover, let rise in warm draft-free place, until double in bulk, about 35 minutes.

Stir down. Spread dough evenly in two 9x5x3-inch loaf pans. Cover; let rise in warm place until double, about 40 minutes.

Combine egg white and cold water; carefully brush tops of loaves. Sprinkle with poppy seed. Heat oven to 375 degrees. Bake for about 45 minutes. Remove from pans and cool on wire rack.

Yield: 2 loaves.

Grandma Salo's Nissua
(Finnish Coffee Bread)
"not a sweet bread — recipe is over 100 years old"

2 packages active dry yeast	½ cup butter or margarine, melted
½ cup warm water (105-115 degrees)	1 teaspoon salt
4 eggs	2 tablespoons cardamom
¾ cup sugar	5 cups all-purpose flour
1½ cups lukewarm milk	

Dissolve yeast in water. In large bowl, beat eggs until frothy and lemon-colored. Add sugar; continue beating. Add yeast mixture, milk and butter; beat well. Add salt, cardamom and flour in 2 additions. Mix well.

Turn out onto floured surface; knead until smooth and elastic. Place dough in well-greased large container and allow to rise in warm place until double in bulk, about 2 hours.

Turn out on lightly floured surface and knead well. Shape dough into 2 round loaves. Place in greased 9-inch pie pans. Let rise in warm place until double, about 1 hour.

Heat oven to 400 degrees. Bake for 40 minutes.

Yield: 2 large loaves.

Variation: Dough may be shaped into twists, braids or buns; bake on cookie sheet for 30 minutes.

Double Dilly Bread
"quickly made"

1 loaf frozen white bread dough, thawed	2 teaspoons finely minced onion
2 tablespoons margarine, melted	½ teaspoon dill weed

Cut off one third of bread dough lengthwise; set aside. Cut remaining two-thirds of dough lengthwise into 3 pieces. Roll each piece into 14-inch rope; braid on greased cookie sheet.

Combine margarine, onion and dill weed. Spoon half of mixture over braid. Cut remaining dough lengthwise into 3 pieces. Roll into ropes and braid. Place on top of large braid. Spoon remaining onion-dill mixture on top. Cover; let rise in warm place until double in bulk.

Heat oven to 375 degrees. Bake for about 25 minutes.

Yield: 1 large braid.

Vasilopita

(Greek New Year's Bread)

"Salt-free traditional Greek bread served on New Year's Day. When baked with a coin hidden inside, the person receiving the slice with the coin will have good luck in the New Year."

1 package active dry yeast	2 eggs, beaten
2 tablespoons warm water	¼ teaspoon cinnamon
(105-115 degrees)	¼ teaspoon nutmeg
⅔ cup warm milk	¼ teaspoon ground cloves
1 teaspoon sugar	¼ cup butter, melted
3 cups all-purpose flour	1 egg, beaten
½ cup sugar	2 tablespoons sesame seed

Dissolve yeast in water. Combine with milk and 1 teaspoon sugar. Stir in ½ cup flour. Cover and let rise in warm place for 1 hour.

Add ½ cup sugar, 2 eggs and spices to butter; stir into dough. Stir in remaining flour. Knead on floured surface until smooth and elastic. Place in oiled bowl, turning to cover with oil. Cover and let double in bulk, about 1½ hours.

Divide dough into thirds and roll each portion into 18-inch rope. Braid loosely on greased cookie sheet. Cover and let rise until double, about 1 hour.

Brush with egg and sprinkle with sesame seed. Heat oven to 375 degrees. Bake for 25-35 minutes.

Yield: 1 braid.

Garlic Bubble Loaf

"break off chunks, eat without butter"

1 loaf frozen white bread dough,	½ teaspoon garlic powder
thawed	1 teaspoon parsley flakes
¼ cup margarine, melted	¼ teaspoon salt
1 egg, beaten	

Cut bread dough into small cubes; shape into balls the size of small walnuts. Combine remaining ingredients. Coat balls of dough in margarine mixture. Place in well greased 9x5x3-inch loaf pan in layers. Cover; let rise in warm place until dough reaches top of pan.

Heat oven to 375 degrees. Bake about 30 minutes. Remove from pan; cool on wire rack.

Yield: 1 loaf.

Rotunda Rye Bread
"a favorite around the Capitol"

1⅓ cups stout or dark ale
⅓ cup butter
⅔ cup corn syrup
2 packages active dry yeast
¼ cup warm water
   (105-115 degrees)
1 teaspoon salt

½ teaspoon ground cloves
¼ teaspoon ginger
2 tablespoons ground orange peel
1½ cups white bread flour
About 3 cups rye flour
Melted butter

Heat stout to boiling; simmer 1 minute. Add butter and corn syrup; cool to lukewarm. Dissolve yeast in water; let stand 5 minutes.

Add yeast, salt, spices, orange peel and white flour to stout. Stir well. Add rye flour gradually until stiff enough to knead. Knead on lightly floured surface until smooth and elastic. Put in greased bowl; cover and let rise in warm place until double in bulk.

Shape into 2 round loaves. Put into 2 greased 8- or 9-inch round pans. Brush tops and sides with melted butter. Cover and let rise until double in bulk.

Heat oven to 350 degrees. Bake for 1 hour. After 30 minutes, brush quickly with water. Do this several more times as baking continues. Remove from pans and cool on wire rack.

Yield: 2 loaves.

Caramel Rolls
"for your sweet-toothed constituency"

2 (1 pound) loaves frozen bread
   dough, partially thawed
½ cup margarine
1 cup packed brown sugar

1 (5⅜ oz.) package vanilla
   pudding and pie filling mix
   (not instant)
1½ teaspoons milk

Divide 1 loaf into 16 pieces; roll into balls and space balls evenly in greased 13x9x2-inch pan.

Combine margarine, brown sugar, pudding mix and milk in saucepan over medium heat; stir until completely blended and margarine is melted. Pour over dough in pan. Divide second loaf into 16 equal pieces and shape into balls. Place in pan, filling up remaining spaces. Let rise about 4-8 hours until doubled in size.

Heat oven to 350 degrees. Bake for 30 minutes. Remove from pan, turning upside down onto cookie sheet. Let cool 15 minutes before serving.

Yield: 16 rolls.

Variation: Substitute butterscotch pudding mix for vanilla; add nuts or raisins.

American Grissini

"Our family lived in northern Italy for a year and enjoyed the thin grissini, bread sticks, of the region. When we returned to the United States, I developed this recipe and technique for making them."

1 package active dry yeast
¼ cup warm water
 (105-115 degrees)
1 cup warm milk
 (110-120 degrees)
¼ cup butter or margarine

1½ tablespoons sugar
½ teaspoon salt
About 3¾ cups all-purpose flour
1 egg white
Butter
Salt

Dissolve yeast in water; let stand 5 minutes. In large bowl, combine milk, ¼ cup butter, sugar and ½ teaspoon salt. Add yeast to milk mixture. Stir in 2 cups flour.

Whip egg white until frothy; add to flour mixture. Work in remaining flour, kneading until dough is smooth and elastic on lightly floured surface. Cover and let rise in warm place until double in bulk.

Working with one-third of dough at a time, roll into a 8x12-inch rectangle about ⅜ inch thick. With a pizza cutter, cut into strips 8x⅜ inches. Lift each strip and stretch slightly lengthwise; place strips ½ inch apart on lightly greased cookie sheet.

Heat oven to 350 degrees. Bake for about 10 minutes until light brown. Remove from oven and immediately brush with butter and sprinkle with salt. Cool on wire rack.

Yield: about 80 grissini.

Pumpkin Pan Rolls

"A generous amount of spice enhances these fine-textured yeast rolls."

1 package active dry yeast
1 cup warm water
 (105-115 degrees)
½ cup sugar
3 tablespoons margarine, melted
1 teaspoon salt
½ cup nonfat dry milk

1 cup canned pumpkin
1½ teaspoons ground cinnamon
¾ teaspoon ground cloves
¾ teaspoon nutmeg
¾ teaspoon ginger
About 5 cups all-purpose flour

In large mixer bowl, soften yeast in water about 5 minutes. Add sugar, margarine, salt, dry milk, pumpkin and spices. Beat at low speed for 2 minutes, then beat in 2 cups flour. With hands, work in 2 more cups flour.

Place dough on surface sprinkled with ½ cup flour; knead dough until smooth, about 15 minutes, adding more flour as needed. Place in greased bowl; cover and let rise in warm place until double, 1½-2 hours.

Punch down and divide dough into 32 equal pieces. Form each piece into a ball. Place balls in 2 greased 9-inch round pans. Cover and let rise until double, about 1 hour.

Heat oven to 375 degrees. Bake for 25 minutes or until browned.

Yield: 32 rolls.

Sticky Buns
"a right-to-be-raised bread"

1 package active dry yeast	Topping:
¼ cup warm water	1 tablespoon light corn syrup
(105-115 degrees)	⅓ cup butter, melted
1 cup warm milk	½ cup packed brown sugar
(105-115 degrees)	½ cup chopped pecans
¼ cup shortening	
¼ cup granulated sugar	Filling:
1 teaspoon salt	¼ cup butter, melted
2 eggs, beaten	⅓ cup granulated sugar
3½ cups all-purpose flour	2 teaspoons cinnamon

Dissolve yeast in water. Combine with remaining bread ingredients, except flour. Gradually stir in flour to form a soft dough. Beat vigorously. Cover with damp cloth and let rise in warm place until double in bulk, about 2 hours.

Turn out on lightly floured surface. Knead dough slightly. Cover; let rest for 10 minutes.

Meanwhile, combine topping ingredients; spread over bottom of greased 13x9x2-inch pan and greased 8x8x2-inch pan.

Place dough on floured surface and roll into a rectangle, about ¼-inch thick. Spread dough with ¼ cup melted butter. Combine sugar and cinnamon; sprinkle over butter. Roll as jelly roll and cut in 18 pieces. Place cut side down on topping in pans. Let rise until double, about 45 minutes.

Bake at 375 degrees for 20 minutes. Invert onto waxed paper.

Yield: 18 rolls.

Icelandic Coffee Bread
"an old recipe from my Icelandic grandmother"

2 packages active dry yeast
½ cup warm water
    (105-115 degrees)
2 cups warm milk
½ cup butter
1 cup sugar
1 teaspoon salt

1½ teaspoons ground cardamom
2 eggs, beaten
1½ cups mixed candied fruit
8½ cups all-purpose flour
½ cup melted butter
½ cup sugar
1 teaspoon cinnamon

Dissolve yeast in water. In large bowl, combine milk, butter, 1 cup sugar, salt and cardamom; stir until sugar is dissolved. Add yeast, eggs and candied fruit. Add flour gradually to make a soft dough. Knead on lightly floured surface until smooth and elastic. Cover and let rise in warm place until double. Punch down; let rise again.

Divide dough in half; cut each half in 3 strips. Shape into ropes and braid on large greased cookie sheet. Cover and let rise until almost double. Brush with melted butter; combine ½ cup sugar and cinnamon; sprinkle on braids.

Heat oven to 350 degrees. Bake for 40 minutes.

Yield: 2 large braids.

Orange Cranberry Bread
"make ahead and freeze"

2 cups all-purpose flour
1½ teaspoons baking powder
1 teaspoon salt
¾ cup sugar
½ teaspoon baking soda
¼ cup margarine

¾ cup orange juice
1 tablespoon grated orange peel
1 egg, well beaten
½ cup chopped nuts
1 cup chopped cranberries

Heat oven to 350 degrees. Stir dry ingredients together. Cut margarine into dry ingredients.

Mix juice and peel with egg; pour all at once into dry ingredients. Mix just to dampen dry ingredients. Add nuts and cranberries.

Pour into greased 9x5x3-inch loaf pan. Bake for 1 hour.

Yield: 1 loaf.

Cranberry Pecan Bread
"The returns are in. This is a winner."

2 cups all-purpose flour
1 teaspoon baking soda
1 teaspoon salt
¾ cups sugar
⅓ cup orange juice
1 teaspoon grated orange peel

3 tablespoons white vinegar
1 egg, slightly beaten
¼ cup shortening, melted
1 cup fresh cranberries, chopped
1 cup pecans, chopped

Heat oven to 350 degrees. Stir dry ingredients together in a large bowl. In a liquid measuring cup, put juice, peel, vinegar and enough water to make ⅔ cup. Mix together juice mixture, egg and shortening.

Add liquid ingredients to dry ingredients and stir just until dry ingredients are moistened. Stir in cranberries and pecans.

Pour batter into a well-greased, lightly-floured 9x5x3-inch loaf pan. Bake for 1-1¼ hours. Allow to cool completely before cutting.

Yield: 1 loaf.

Seven Week Bran Muffins
"always on the agenda"

3 cups whole bran cereal
1 cup boiling water
½ cup vegetable oil
2½ cups all-purpose flour
2½ teaspoons baking soda
1 teaspoon salt

2 eggs, slightly beaten
1½ cups sugar
2 cups buttermilk
1½ cups pitted and chopped
   dates (optional)

Mix 1 cup bran cereal and boiling water; cool. Mix in oil.

In large bowl, mix remaining ingredients except dates. Combine mixtures, stirring well. Stir in dates. Cover and refrigerate.

When ready to use, heat oven to 400 degrees. Fill greased muffin cups ⅔ full. Bake for 25-30 minutes.

This batter may be refrigerated for 7 weeks and used as needed.

Yield: 36 muffins.

Appleside Cinnamon Muffins

"your own apples are the best natural resource"

2 cups all-purpose flour
4 teaspoons baking powder
½ teaspoon salt
¼ cup sugar
½ teaspoon cinnamon

¼ cup shortening, melted
1 cup milk
1 egg, slightly beaten
1 cup unpeeled chopped apple
¼ cup sugar

Heat oven to 350 degrees. Stir flour, baking powder, salt, ¼ cup sugar and cinnamon together. Combine shortening, milk and egg; add to dry ingredients, blending just until ingredients are moistened.

Combine apples and ¼ cup sugar and stir into batter.

Fill well-greased muffin cups ⅔ full. Bake for 35 minutes.

Yield: 18 muffins.

Dark Cherry Muffins

"Yes! you use sherbet."

3 cups buttermilk biscuit mix
1 egg, beaten
2 cups lemon or pineapple
   sherbet, softened

1 (16 oz.) package frozen dark
   pitted cherries, thawed,
   drained and coarsely chopped
1 teaspoon cinnamon
2 teaspoons sugar

Heat oven to 375 degrees. Combine biscuit mix and egg; gradually stir in sherbet. Stir in cherries. Combine cinnamon and sugar.

Fill greased muffin cups ¾ full; sprinkle with cinnamon-sugar mixture. Bake for 15-20 minutes.

Yield: 16 muffins.

Banana-Oatmeal Muffins

"Nutritious — and they disappear too fast to freeze!"

6 tablespoons vegetable oil	1 teaspoon baking powder
2 eggs	1 teaspoon baking soda
4 medium bananas, mashed	¾ teaspoon salt
½ cup honey	1 cup rolled oats
1½ cups whole wheat flour	

Heat oven to 375 degrees. Mix together oil, eggs, bananas and honey. Stir together dry ingredients; add to liquid mixture, stirring until just blended. Fill greased muffin cups ⅔ full. Bake for 18-20 minutes.

Yield: 24 muffins.

Dining Car Blueberry Muffins

"when the campaign train rolls in"

1 cup sugar	1 tablespoon baking powder
½ cup butter, softened	¾ teaspoon salt
3 eggs	1 cup milk
3 cups all-purpose flour	2 cups blueberries

Heat oven to 400 degrees. Cream sugar and butter in large mixing bowl. Add eggs and beat thoroughly.

Stir together flour, baking powder and salt. Add alternately with milk to creamed mixture. Fold in blueberries.

Fill greased muffin cups ⅔ full. Bake for 20 minutes.

Yield: 24 muffins.

Cranberry Bog Coffee Cake

"enjoyed on both sides of the aisle"

2 eggs, slightly beaten	1½ cups biscuit mix
½ cup sugar	1 (8 oz.) can cranberry jelly, cut
½ teaspoon salt	into ½-inch cubes
½ teaspoon nutmeg	1 cup pecans, chopped
1 tablespoon lemon juice	

Heat oven to 350 degrees. Combine eggs, sugar, salt, nutmeg, lemon juice and biscuit mix. Gently fold in cranberry jelly and pecans.

Spread batter in greased 9x9x2-inch pan. Bake for 25 minutes.

Yield: 36 bars.

Swedish Hardtack

"won't get a chance to be stored"

2 cups buttermilk
1½ teaspoons baking soda
1 cup vegetable oil
½ cup sugar

1 cup rolled oats
1 tablespoon salt
2½ cups whole wheat flour
1-1¼ cups all-purpose flour

Heat oven to 375 degrees. Combine ingredients in order listed.

Divide dough into thirds. Using a Swedish or regular rolling pin, roll each part of dough out on a lightly floured board to ⅛-inch thickness.

Bake on an ungreased cookie sheet for 7-10 minutes. Turn dough and bake an additional 7-10 minutes. Both sides should be brown.

Cool. Break into pieces and store in airtight container.

Yield: Three 11x14-inch cookie sheets full.

Halloween Corn Bread

"Excellent flavor — beautiful golden color."

1¼ cups all-purpose flour
1 tablespoon baking powder
⅓ cup packed brown sugar
½ teaspoon salt
¾ teaspoon ginger

¾ cup cornmeal
2 eggs, slightly beaten
¼ cup margarine, melted
⅔ cup buttermilk
¾ cup cooked, mashed squash

Heat oven to 350 degrees. Stir dry ingredients together. Mix eggs, margarine, buttermilk and squash together. Add all at once to dry ingredients, stirring just until dry ingredients are moistened.

Pour into greased 8x8x2-inch baking pan or fill greased muffin cups ⅔ full. Bake bread for 35-40 minutes or muffins for 30-35 minutes.

Yield: One 8x8x2-inch bread or 1 dozen muffins.

Danish Puff

"This will look like a flat cream puff."

½ cup butter
1 cup all-purpose flour
2 tablespoons water
1 cup water
½ cup butter
1 teaspoon almond extract
1 cup all-purpose flour
3 eggs

Icing:
1 cup powdered sugar
1 tablespoon butter or margarine, softened
½ teaspoon almond extract
2-3 tablespoons milk
Sliced almonds or grated coconut

Heat oven to 350 degrees. Cut ½ cup butter into 1 cup flour; add 2 tablespoons water and mix as for pie crust. Divide dough in half. Pat into strips (12x3 inches) on ungreased cookie sheet.

In medium saucepan, bring 1 cup water and ½ cup butter to boil. Remove from heat; quickly add 1 teaspoon extract and 1 cup flour. Stir until a ball is formed and follows spoon. Add eggs one at a time, beating well after each. Divide and spread over pastry strips. Bake for 50-60 minutes. Cool.

For icing, blend all ingredients together until smooth. Spread on cooled puffs; sprinkle with sliced nuts.

Yield: 16-20 slices.

Variation: Substitute melted fruit jelly for icing.

Oat Scones

"a traditional Irish recipe"

1 cup all-purpose flour
1 cup rolled oats
½ teaspoon salt
½ teaspoon baking soda

1 teaspoon cream of tartar
1 tablespoon sugar
¼ cup shortening
½ cup milk or buttermilk

Heat oven to 425 degrees. Stir dry ingredients together in mixing bowl. Cut in shortening. Add milk and stir with fork to form a soft dough.

Pat dough into well-greased 8- or 9-inch round cake pan.

Using a knife, score dough into 8 wedges. Bake for 15 minutes.

Yield: 8 scones.

Overnight Coffee Cake
"perfect for a morning meeting"

2 cups all-purpose flour
½ teaspoon salt
1 teaspoon baking soda
1 teaspoon baking powder
¾ cup margarine, softened
½ cup granulated sugar
½ cup packed brown sugar

1 teaspoon vanilla
2 eggs, beaten
1 cup buttermilk
½ cup packed brown sugar
1 teaspoon cinnamon
½ teaspoon nutmeg
½ cup nuts, chopped (optional)

Stir together flour, salt, baking soda and baking powder; set aside. Cream margarine with granulated sugar, ½ cup brown sugar and vanilla until light and fluffy. Add eggs and beat again until fluffy. Add flour mixture alternately with buttermilk.

Pour into greased 13x9x2-inch pan. Mix ½ cup brown sugar, cinnamon, nutmeg and nuts together. Sprinkle evenly over top of cake. Cover and refrigerate overnight. Heat oven to 350 degrees; uncover coffee cake and bake for 35 minutes.

Yield: 10-12 servings.

Kropsu
(Finnish Oven Pancake)
"try with a fruit sauce"

4 eggs
¼ cup honey
¾ teaspoon salt

2½ cups milk
1 cup all-purpose flour
¼ cup margarine, softened

Heat oven to 400 degrees. Place 13x9x2-inch pan in oven for 10 minutes. Melt margarine in heated pan.

In glass bowl, beat eggs until fluffy. Add honey, salt, milk and flour, beating until well blended. Slowly add batter to pan.

Bake for 35 minutes, until top is golden brown and batter has risen like a popover.

Yield: 5-6 servings.

Tea Pancakes and Lemon Curd

"a prize-winning recipe from Dunoon, Scotland"

2 cups self-rising flour*
¾ cup sugar
1 teaspoon baking soda
1 teaspoon cream of tartar

2 eggs, slightly beaten
1 cup milk
3 tablespoons butter
Lemon Curd (below)

Stir dry ingredients together. Stir in eggs; add milk to make a smooth batter about the consistency of thick cream. Drop batter to form 3-inch pancakes on a buttered hot skillet. Serve with Lemon Curd.

*If self-rising flour is not available, substitute 2 cups flour, 3 teaspoons baking powder and 1 teaspoon salt for the 2 cups self-rising flour.

Yield: about 3 dozen (3-inch) pancakes.

Lemon Curd:

6 eggs
½ cup butter
2 cups sugar

Grated peel of 2 lemons
Juice of 3 lemons

Beat eggs until light and fluffy. Mix remaining ingredients in saucepan. Place over low heat and cook until sugar dissolves, stirring constantly. Remove from heat.

Add beaten eggs to lemon mixture. Return to heat and cook over low heat, stirring constantly until mixture coats a metal spoon. Do not boil. Mixture will be the consistency of honey. Refrigerate.

Yield: about 3½ cups.

Purposeful Pancakes

"handle with care — cakes are delicate"

¾ cup unbleached flour
½ cup whole wheat flour
¼ cup wheat germ
2 tablespoons bran
2 teaspoons brewer's yeast
1 teaspoon baking powder
½ teaspoon baking soda
½ teaspoon salt

1 tablespoon sugar or honey
¾-1 cup rolled oats
1 egg, slightly beaten
2 cups buttermilk
¼ cup vegetable oil
Roasted sesame seeds
Hot Spiced Applesauce (below)

Stir together dry ingredients. Combine egg, buttermilk, oil and honey (if used); add to dry ingredients, beating until well blended.

Pour 4-inch pancakes onto lightly greased griddle on medium-low heat; sprinkle batter with sesame seeds. Bake until golden brown. Serve with Hot Spiced Applesauce.

Yield: 16 (4-inch) pancakes.

Hot Spiced Applesauce:

2 cups applesauce
1 teaspoon cinnamon

¼ teaspoon allspice
2 teaspoons honey

Combine all ingredients; heat.

SALADS ✓

Lemon Chiffon Ring with Fresh Fruit

"delicate lemon flavor"

2 envelopes unflavored gelatin
½ cup cold water
⅔ cup sugar
⅔ cup lemon juice
6 eggs, separated

⅛ teaspoon salt
2 teaspoons lemon peel
½ cup sugar
Grapes and strawberries

Soften gelatin in cold water. Mix ⅔ cup sugar and lemon juice together. In small bowl, beat egg yolks with salt until thick and light yellow in color.

Mix beaten yolks, sugar and lemon juice together in top of double boiler.Cook, stirring constantly, until mixture coats a metal spoon. Remove from heat and stir in gelatin and lemon peel. Refrigerate until thickened.

In large bowl, beat egg whites until very soft peaks form. Gradually beat in ½ cup sugar. Continue beating until stiff peaks form. Fold egg whites gently into gelatin mixture until well blended. Pour into a 2-quart ring mold. Refrigerate several hours until firm.

Unmold and fill center with grapes and strawberries.

Yield: 12 servings.

Variation: For a dessert ring, frost with whipped cream to which chopped mint has been added.

Banana Gelatin Salad

"gels while you register voters"

1 envelope unflavored gelatin
¼ cup cold water
½ cup boiling water
¼ cup sugar
1¼ cups orange juice
1½ tablespoons lime juice

1½ cups mashed bananas
(about 3)
2 tablespoons lemon juice
1 tablespoon fruit preservative
½ cup chopped walnuts

Soften gelatin in cold water. Dissolve in boiling water. Add sugar, orange juice and lime juice. Refrigerate until slightly thickened.

Combine mashed bananas, lemon juice and fruit preservative. Stir into gelatin mixture. Add nuts. Pour into 4-cup mold. Chill until firm.

Unmold and garnish with greens and fruits of your choice.

Yield: 6 (½-cup) servings.

Orange-Apricot Salad
"smooth and creamy"

1 (17 oz.) can apricot halves, drained; reserve 1 cup juice
½ cup orange juice

1 (3 oz.) package orange-flavored gelatin
Apricot Dressing (below)

Purée apricots and orange juice in blender or food processor.

Heat reserved apricot juice to boiling; add gelatin and stir to dissolve. Stir in apricot purée; pour into 8x8x2-inch pan or 8 individual molds. Refrigerate until firm.

Unmold and serve with Apricot Dressing.

Yield: 8 servings.

Apricot Dressing:

¼ cup mayonnaise
⅓ cup apricot preserves

¼ cup plain yogurt

Combine mayonnaise, preserves and yogurt. Serve as salad dressing or dip with fresh fruit.

Yield: ¾ cup.

Olive Wreath Mold
"good accompaniment to spring lamb"

1 (20 oz.) can crushed pineapple, drained, reserve juice
1 (3 oz.) package lime-flavored gelatin
½ cup (2 oz.) shredded Cheddar cheese
½ cup finely chopped celery

⅔ cup chopped walnuts
¼ teaspoon salt
½ cup chopped pimiento
½ cup whipping cream, whipped
1 (2 oz.) jar pimiento-stuffed green olives

Heat reserved pineapple juice to boiling; add gelatin and stir until dissolved. Refrigerate until the consistency of thick egg white.

Add remaining ingredients except whipped cream and olives. Fold in whipped cream.

Slice olives and place on bottom of 2-quart ring mold or bundt pan. Carefully pour mixture into mold and refrigerate until firm.

Yield: 8 servings.

Festive Frozen Cranberry Salad

"make this ahead for holiday entertaining"

1 (14 oz.) can sweetened
   condensed milk
¼ cup lemon juice
1 (16 oz.) can whole berry
   cranberry sauce
½ cup chopped nuts or coconut

1 (20 oz.) can crushed
   pineapple, drained
1 (9 oz.) container frozen
   non-dairy whipped topping,
   thawed
Lettuce leaves

In large bowl, combine sweetened condensed milk and lemon juice. Stir in cranberry sauce, nuts and pineapple. Fold in whipped topping.

Spread in 13x9x2-inch pan. Freeze until firm. Remove from freezer 10 minutes before cutting. Serve on lettuce.

Yield: 15 servings.

Winter Fruit Salad

"some fresh — some canned"

2 (20 oz.) cans pineapple chunks,
   drained; reserve juice
2 (11 oz.) cans mandarin oranges,
   drained

4 medium unpeeled apples,
   chopped
4 bananas, sliced
Cooked Juice Dressing (below)

Combine fruit in a bowl; pour hot Cooked Juice Dressing over fruit. Refrigerate uncovered for several hours.

Yield: 12 servings.

Cooked Juice Dressing:

1½ cups reserved pineapple juice
1 tablespoon sugar
¼ cup cornstarch

2 tablespoons fresh lemon juice
⅔ cup orange juice

In saucepan, mix sugar and cornstarch; add juices. Cook, stirring constantly, until thick and boiling. Boil 1 minute.

Yield: about 2½ cups.

Sunday Salad
"a long forgotten, simple recipe"

1 small head lettuce
1 apple, diced
1 banana, diced

3 tablespoons sugar
2 tablespoons vinegar
¼ cup half and half cream

Shred lettuce. Sprinkle apple and banana over lettuce. Combine remaining ingredients; pour over salad.

Yield: 4 servings.

Butter Lettuce with Walnut Oil Dressing
"No substitutions! Worth the search for these ingredients."

½ cup chopped walnuts
1 (14 oz.) can hearts of palm

2 heads butterhead lettuce*
Walnut Oil Dressing (below)

Toast walnuts at 350 degrees until lightly browned. Drain hearts of palm; cut into 1-inch pieces.

Combine lettuce, hearts of palm and walnuts in salad bowl. Toss enough Walnut Oil Dressing with salad to moisten.

*Butterhead lettuce is Boston or bibb.

Yield: 8 servings.

Walnut Oil Dressing:

⅔ cup walnut oil*
¼ cup minced green onion
1 tablespoon Dijon mustard
1-2 teaspoons sugar

6 tablespoons red wine vinegar
Salt and freshly ground pepper
to taste

Combine ingredients in covered jar; shake well.

*Walnut oil can be purchased at health food and some grocery stores.

Yield: about 1⅓ cups.

Hot Spinach Salad

"add your own garnish"

6 slices bacon, diced
12 cups spinach or romaine,
  torn in bite-size pieces
1 medium onion, diced
Pepper to taste
½ teaspoon sugar
3 tablespoons wine vinegar

½ teaspoon Dijon mustard
6 tablespoons whipping cream
2 hard-cooked eggs, diced
Sunflower nuts, sautéed in
  bacon drippings
Garlic Croutons
Tiny Cheddar cheese cubes

Fry bacon until crisp; drain and reserve 5 tablespoons drippings. Place spinach in serving bowl. Sprinkle onion on top. Chill.

When ready to serve salad, season with pepper and sugar. Reheat bacon and reserved drippings. Combine vinegar and mustard; add to bacon all at once. Cover skillet momentarily to prevent spattering. Lift lid and pour mixture over spinach. Turn hot skillet upside down over spinach; leave for a minute to wilt slightly. Add cream and toss salad.

Garnish with eggs, sunflower nuts, croutons and cheese.

Yield: 6 servings.

Marinated Asparagus Bouquet

"by acclamation"

3 (10 oz.) packages frozen
  asparagus spears
1 medium Bermuda onion,
  finely chopped
Salt and pepper to taste

Piquant Dressing (below)
Lettuce leaves
1 (4 oz.) jar sliced pimiento
½ cup chopped fresh parsley

Cook asparagus according to package directions until tender; do not overcook. Drain well.

Arrange in single layer in shallow non-metallic dish. Spread chopped onion over top; season with salt and pepper. Drizzle Piquant Dressing evenly over asparagus. Refrigerate for several hours or overnight.

To serve, drain asparagus and place an equal number of spears on each plate lined with lettuce. Top with strips of pimiento placed diagonally across spears. Sprinkle with parsley.

Yield: 10 servings.

Piquant Dressing:

1 cup vegetable oil
½ cup vinegar
2 tablespoons sugar
1 teaspoon salt

½ teaspoon dry mustard
½ teaspoon celery seed
1 small clove garlic, finely
   chopped

Combine all ingredients in covered jar; shake well.

Yield: about 1⅔ cups.

Fresh Spinach Salad with Lemony-Dill Dressing

"excellent accompaniment to quiche"

1 pound fresh spinach, torn into
   bite-size pieces
2 cups sliced fresh mushrooms
   (about 6 oz.)

½ cup (2 oz.) crumbled feta
   cheese
¼ cup finely chopped
   green onions
Lemony-Dill Dressing (below)

Toss spinach, mushrooms, cheese and onions together in salad bowl; chill 2 hours. Toss salad with Lemony-Dill Dressing before serving.

Yield: 6 servings.

Lemony-Dill Dressing:

1 cup olive oil
¼ teaspoon chopped lemon peel
2 tablespoons lemon juice
1 egg yolk
2 cloves garlic, minced
½ teaspoon salt

½ teaspoon dry mustard
½ teaspoon oregano leaves
¼ teaspoon sugar
⅛ teaspoon freshly ground
   pepper
½ teaspoon dill weed

Combine all ingredients in covered jar; shake well. Chill dressing.

Yield: about 1½ cups.

Cauliflower Salad
"Greek-style"

1 medium head cauliflower	6 green onions, sliced
1 (3 oz.) can ripe olives, drained and sliced	4 medium tomatoes, quartered
	Elysian Dressing (below)
1 large green pepper, cut in small strips	¼ cup (1 oz.) feta cheese

Wash and separate cauliflower into flowerets. Steam until crisp-tender, about 5 minutes. Plunge into cold water; drain.

Combine cauliflower, olives, green pepper, onions and tomatoes in bowl. Pour Elysian Dressing over vegetables. Marinate 4 hours in refrigerator. Crumble feta cheese on top.

Yield: 4-6 servings.

Elysian Dressing:

9 tablespoons olive oil	½ teaspoon minced garlic
3 tablespoons red wine vinegar	½ teaspoon oregano leaves
1 tablespoon Dijon mustard (optional)	Freshly ground pepper to taste
½ teaspoon salt	

Combine all ingredients in covered jar; shake well.

Yield: about ¾ cup.

Su No Mono
"no 'sunset' for this Rising Sun salad"

2 small cucumbers	¼ cup white vinegar
1 carrot	¼ cup sugar
1 teaspoon salt	

Peel cucumbers, leaving strips of skin on for color. Cut in half lengthwise; remove seeds and slice very thin. Peel carrot; cut 5 V-shaped grooves lengthwise in carrot. Cut crosswise into very thin slices. Grooves will make petal shapes so carrot slices look like flowers.

Place cucumbers and carrots in colander and sprinkle with salt. Let stand for 15 minutes. Stir vinegar and sugar together until sugar is dissolved. Squeeze cucumbers and carrots; add to vinegar-sugar mixture. Marinate at least 4 hours in refrigerator, stirring once or twice.

Sliced radishes may be added for more color or to increase amount of salad.

Yield: 6 servings.

Creamy Cole Slaw
"You'll cross the aisle for this."

½ medium head cabbage,
   chopped (about 2½ cups)
1 carrot, shredded
1 teaspoon salt
3 tablespoons mayonnaise

1 tablespoon sugar
1 teaspoon grated onion
1 tablespoon vinegar
6 tablespoons whipping cream
1 tablespoon mustard

Combine cabbage and carrot. Combine remaining ingredients; toss with cabbage. Refrigerate at least 2 hours before serving.

Yield: 6 servings

Uncle Sam Salad
"a standby for pot-luck suppers"

1 pound mostaccioli noodles
   or other large pasta
1-2 cucumbers, diced
1 large tomato, diced

1 medium onion, diced
1 green pepper, diced
Sweet Herb Dressing (below)

Cook mostaccioli according to package directions; drain and cool. Add cucumbers, tomato, onion and green pepper. Pour some Sweet Herb Dressing over salad to moisten. Refrigerate several hours.

Yield: 5 quarts. (Fills large plastic ice cream bucket.)

Sweet Herb Dressing:

1½ cups vegetable oil
1¼ cups vinegar
½ cup sugar
1½ teaspoons instant
   minced onion
2 teaspoons salt

¾ teaspoon pepper
2 teaspoons prepared mustard
1 teaspoon garlic powder
½ teaspoon celery seed
2 tablespoons chopped parsley

Combine all ingredients in covered jar; shake well.

Yield: about 2½ cups.

Marinated Fresh Vegetables

"The crowd concurs. This is great."

1 head cauliflower
1 head broccoli
1 (7 oz.) can pitted ripe olives, drained
8-16 oz. fresh mushrooms, sliced
1 small onion, grated

1 cup (4 oz.) shredded mozzarella cheese
1 (10 oz.) package frozen peas, thawed
Honey-Herb Dressing (below)

Cut cauliflower and broccoli into bite-size pieces. Combine with remaining ingredients and refrigerate at least 8 hours; stir several times.

Yield: 8-12 servings.

Honey-Herb Dressing:

1 teaspoon garlic powder
1 teaspoon salt
½ teaspoon black pepper
½ teaspoon dry mustard
½ teaspoon sweet basil

½ teaspoon oregano
½ teaspoon paprika
⅔ cup red wine vinegar
1 tablespoon honey
1½ cups safflower or corn oil

Mix seasonings in small jar with cover. Add vinegar and let stand to soften herbs. Add honey and oil; cover and shake vigorously.

Yield: about 2¼ cups.

Taco Salad

"transports well"

1 pound ground beef
1 envelope dry onion soup mix
1 cup water
1 small head lettuce, chopped
1 cup halved cherry tomatoes

1 (8 oz.) bag taco chips, crushed
1 cup (4 oz.) shredded Cheddar cheese
Taco sauce

Brown ground beef in skillet; drain. Add soup mix and water; simmer 20 minutes.

Put lettuce in large bowl; add tomatoes. Refrigerate.

Just before serving, sprinkle taco chips and cheese over lettuce mixture; pour warm ground beef mixture over all. Toss to combine. Serve with taco sauce.

Yield: 6-8 servings.

Summer Salad
"prepare early on a hot summer day"

1 cup diced cooked chicken
  or ham
½ cup (2 oz.) diced Cheddar
  cheese

2 cups cooked, diced potatoes
Poppy Seed Dressing (below)
½ cantaloupe, cut into balls
½ honeydew melon, cut into balls

Gently toss meat, cheese and potatoes together with enough Poppy Seed Dressing to moisten; chill. Add melon balls to salad just before serving.

Yield: 6 servings.

Poppy Seed Dressing:

1 clove garlic
1 cup vegetable oil
⅓ cup white wine vinegar
2 tablespoons honey

1 teaspoon salt
⅛ teaspoon pepper
1 tablespoon poppy seed

Whirl all ingredients together in blender.

Yield: about 1½ cups.

Chilled Chicken Salad Pie
"beautiful luncheon or supper dish"

3 (5 oz.) cans boned chicken,
  drained and flaked
1 (13½ oz.) can crushed
  pineapple, drained
1½ cups (6 oz.) shredded
  Cheddar cheese
1 cup diced celery

¾ cup sliced almonds
¾ cup mayonnaise
9-inch baked pie shell
1 cup whipping cream, whipped
2 tablespoons mayonnaise
Shredded carrot

Combine chicken, pineapple, cheese, celery, almonds and ¾ cup mayonnaise. Spoon into pie shell; refrigerate.

Combine whipped cream and 2 tablespoons mayonnaise; spoon on top of pie. Garnish with carrot.

Yield: 8 servings.

Curried Chicken Cantaloupe Salad

"exotic and light"

1 small cantaloupe
1 cup cubed cooked chicken
½ cup halved green grapes
½ cup sliced celery

Curry Dressing (below)
2 tablespoons slivered
almonds, toasted

Using a melon ball cutter, cut cantaloupe into balls; save shell. Combine melon balls, chicken, grapes and celery; toss with Curry Dressing. Add almonds just before serving. Serve in cantaloupe shells.

Yield: 2 servings.

Curry Dressing:

½ cup mayonnaise
½ cup dairy sour cream or yogurt
1 teaspoon soy sauce

½ teaspoon curry powder
¼ teaspoon salt

Combine all ingredients. Keep refrigerated until ready to use.

Yield: about 1 cup.

Indonesian Salad

"unanimous choice"

7 cups cooked, diced turkey
2 tablespoons lime juice (optional)
2 cups raisins
2 cups dry roasted peanuts

1 cup flaked coconut
2 cups chopped celery
2 cups chopped green pepper
Chutney Dressing (below)

Marinate turkey in lime juice overnight, if desired. Combine turkey, raisins, peanuts, coconut, celery and green pepper in large serving bowl. Refrigerate until chilled. Serve with Chutney Dressing.

Yield: 10-12 servings.

Chutney Dressing:

1 cup mayonnaise
1 cup yogurt
2 teaspoons lemon juice

½ cup minced onion
1 teaspoon curry powder
3 tablespoons chopped chutney

Combine ingredients and refrigerate at least 4 hours before serving.

Yield: about 2⅔ cups.

Great Zeus Chicken Salad

"food for the gods"

3 whole chicken breasts
¼ cup olive oil
1 clove garlic, minced
¼ teaspoon salt
½ teaspoon cumin
2 tablespoons lemon juice
1½ cups sliced celery
½ cup chopped green onion

½ cup ripe olives, sliced in rings
1 large cucumber, peeled and cubed
1 (11 oz.) can mandarin oranges, drained
Juno's Salad Dressing (below)
Fresh spinach or romaine leaves

Skin, debone and cut chicken into bite-size chunks. Stir-fry in mixture of oil, garlic, salt and cumin until chicken is opaque. Sprinkle chicken with lemon juice; refrigerate.

Just before serving, toss chicken with celery, onion, olives, cucumber and oranges. Pour enough Juno's Salad Dressing over chicken mixture to moisten; toss well. Serve on a bed of spinach leaves.

This is easily prepared ahead in segments and then combined at the last minute.

Yield: 6 servings.

Juno's Salad Dressing:

⅓ cup dairy sour cream
⅓ cup mayonnaise
1 teaspoon basil

½ teaspoon salt
½ teaspoon cumin
Dash of Tabasco sauce

Combine all ingredients. Refrigerate until ready to use.

Yield: about ⅔ cup.

Lentil Salad
"stays within the budget"

2½ cups dried lentils
2 small onions
6 whole cloves
3 carrots, scraped, quartered and sliced
1½ quarts stock or canned chicken broth
2 teaspoons dried thyme

1 bay leaf
⅓ cup white wine vinegar
½ cup olive oil
2 cloves garlic, minced
Coarse salt and freshly ground pepper to taste
1 cup sliced green onions
1 cup walnut pieces (optional)

Rinse and sort lentils. Cut each onion into 3 pieces; stick 1 clove into each onion piece. Combine lentils, onions, carrots, stock, thyme and bay leaf in large pot. Bring to a boil; reduce heat and simmer for 25 minutes. Do not overcook or the lentils will turn mushy.

Beat vinegar, oil and garlic together. Drain lentils, discard bay leaf and cloves. Pour dressing over warm lentils and gently toss, adding salt and pepper. Cool almost to room temperature; refrigerate several hours or overnight. Before serving add onions and walnuts.

"This dish keeps wonderfully for at least 5 days. If you're feeling extravagant, you can prepare it with walnut oil instead of olive oil. Vegetarians will enjoy it as a main luncheon course, lunch-packers will like a small carton in their brown bag, and the dish has been known to be a smash at an otherwise traditional Thanksgiving dinner. Though not a low-calorie item, it is a boon to those who wish to cut down the size of their meals, for it suffices as main course, salad and vegetable all in one. And it is so tasty, especially with herbs and garlic, that it proves extraordinarily satisfying."

Yield: 8-10 servings.

Chef Salad Dressing
"rich and spicy"

½ cup dairy sour cream
½ cup mayonnaise
¼ cup half and half cream
½ teaspoon curry powder
½ teaspoon dry mustard

½ teaspoon Worcestershire sauce
½ teaspoon prepared horseradish
½ teaspoon steak sauce (optional)
1 clove garlic, minced
Salt and white pepper to taste

Combine all ingredients and mix well. Chill several hours or overnight.

Yield: 1¼ cups.

Mrs. Mae's Dressing
"a sweet French Dressing"

½ cup sugar
1 cup vegetable oil
⅓ cup catsup
⅓ cup flavored vinegar

½ teaspoon salt
1 teaspoon celery seed
1 tablespoon paprika
1 onion, minced

Thoroughly combine all ingredients. Cover and refrigerate.

Yield: about 2 cups.

Blender Salad Dressing
"quick and basic dressing for greens with fruit"

¼ cup sugar
2 teaspoons salt
½ teaspoon dry mustard

½ cup white wine vinegar
½ cup vegetable oil
½ cup chopped or sliced onion

Whirl all ingredients in blender until smooth and thickened.

Yield: 1¾ cups.

Zero Salad Dressing
"Dieters will appreciate this tangy dressing."

½ cup tomato juice
2 tablespoons lemon juice or
   vinegar
1 tablespoon finely chopped
   onion

Salt and pepper to taste
Chopped parsley, chopped green
   pepper, horseradish, mustard
   or other herbs of your choice,
   as desired

Combine ingredients in covered jar; shake well.

Yield: about ¾ cup.

Blender Blue Cheese Dressing
"a family favorite"

1 cup vegetable oil
⅓ cup red wine or white
   tarragon vinegar
2 tablespoons mayonnaise
½ teaspoon salt (optional)

½ teaspoon dry mustard
1 clove garlic, crushed
¼ cup (1 oz.) crumbled blue
   cheese

Combine all ingredients in blender. Refrigerate. Dressing will separate on standing; shake well before using.

Yield: 1½ cups.

Herbed Vinaigrette Dressing

"for curry lovers"

⅓ cup white wine vinegar
½ teaspoon salt (optional)
½ teaspoon Dijon mustard
Freshly ground pepper to taste
½ teaspoon parsley
½ teaspoon tarragon
½ teaspoon chives

½ teaspoon chervil
½ teaspoon capers (optional)
⅔ cup vegetable oil
⅓ cup olive oil
1 egg
1 teaspoon curry powder
1-2 teaspoons water

Blend vinegar, salt, mustard, pepper, parsley, tarragon, chives, chervil and capers in blender for 1 minute. Add oils and egg, let stand 1 minute; blend 1 minute. Combine curry powder and water; blend into dressing 1 minute. Refrigerate at least 4 hours before serving.

Yield: 1⅔ cups.

Grandma's Boiled Dressing

"like partisan politics, evokes strong feelings"

¾-1 cup cider vinegar
2 tablespoons butter
1 tablespoon flour
1 tablespoon dry mustard

1 teaspoon salt
⅓ cup sugar
3 eggs, beaten

Heat vinegar and butter in top of double boiler.

Stir flour, mustard, salt and sugar together; add to eggs. Add egg mixture to hot vinegar. Cook, stirring constantly, until thickened and coats a metal spoon (about 5 minutes). Keep refrigerated.

Beat with egg beater if dressing curdles. A very flavorful substitute for mayonnaise in deviled eggs, minced ham, potato salad, etc.

Yield: 2 cups.

Classified Carrots
"orange juice is the secret"

6 (16 oz.) cans small carrots
1 (6 oz.) can frozen orange juice
　　concentrate, thawed
3 tablespoons brown sugar

¼ teaspoon cinnamon
¼ teaspoon nutmeg
1 tablespoon butter

Drain carrots. Mix together orange juice concentrate, brown sugar, cinnamon and nutmeg.

Put carrots in large greased casserole; pour orange sauce over carrots. Dot with butter. Bake at 350 degrees for 30 minutes. Carrots can also be simmered on range with orange mixture until heated through.

Yield: 16 servings.

Caucus Carrots
"a resolution for your vegetable problem"

8 medium carrots, scraped
¼ cup butter
¼ cup canned jellied
　　cranberry sauce

2 tablespoons brown sugar
½ teaspoon salt

Slice carrots ½-inch thick. Cook, covered, in small amount of water until just tender, about 6-10 minutes.

In skillet, combine remaining ingredients. Heat slowly and stir until cranberry sauce melts.

Add drained carrots. Heat, stirring occasionally, until carrots are glazed on all sides, about 5 minutes.

Yield: 6-8 servings.

Broccoli Casserole
"with a creamy cheese sauce"

1 cup uncooked rice
2 (10 oz.) packages frozen
  broccoli spears
½ cup chopped onion
½ cup chopped celery
¼ cup margarine

2 (10¾ oz.) cans condensed
  cream of mushroom soup
¾ cup milk
8 oz. (2 cups) shredded Cheddar
  cheese
2 tablespoons bread crumbs
1 teaspoon vegetable oil

Cook rice according to package directions. Cook broccoli 3 minutes; drain and arrange broccoli in 2-quart casserole.

Sauté onion and celery in margarine until tender. Stir in undiluted soup, milk and rice. Add cheese and stir to blend. Pour mixture over broccoli.

Combine crumbs and oil; sprinkle on top. Bake at 350 degrees for 20-30 minutes.

Yield: 8 servings.

Whole Cauliflower
"a showstopper!"

1 medium head cauliflower
Swiss cheese, cut into cubes
¼ cup butter
¼ cup flour
1 cup milk

½ cup (2 oz.) shredded Swiss
  cheese
½ teaspoon grated nutmeg
½ teaspoon salt
White pepper
Paprika

Cook whole cauliflower in salted water until barely tender, about 15 minutes. Drain and stick cubes of Swiss cheese in among flowerets.

Melt butter in saucepan, stir in flour; gradually add milk. Bring to a boil and cook 1 minute, stirring constantly. Remove from heat. Stir in shredded cheese, nutmeg, salt and pepper.

Pour sauce over cauliflower. Dust with paprika. Just before serving, brown under broiler.

Yield: 6 servings.

Green Beans Supreme
"a favorite from the Minnesota House"

1 pound fresh or 2 (10 oz.)
  packages frozen green beans
2 tablespoons butter
3 tablespoons minced onion
1 tablespoon flour
½ teaspoon salt
½ teaspoon paprika

¼ teaspoon dry mustard
½ teaspoon Worcestershire sauce
1 cup whipping cream
1 cup (4 oz.) shredded Cheddar
  cheese
2 tablespoons dry bread crumbs
1 teaspoon vegetable oil

If using fresh beans, cook 10-15 minutes. Prepare frozen beans according to package directions. Drain beans.

Heat butter in saucepan over low heat. Add onion and cook until transparent. Remove from heat and stir in flour, salt, paprika, dry mustard and Worcestershire sauce. Bring to a boil and cook 1 minute, stirring constantly. Remove from heat.

Add cream gradually, stirring constantly. Return to heat and bring rapidly to boiling, stirring constantly; cook 1-2 minutes longer.

Add beans to sauce. Toss mixture gently with a spoon until blended. Spoon into 1-quart baking dish. Sprinkle with shredded cheese. Combine bread crumbs and oil; sprinkle over cheese.

Broil 2-3 inches from heat for 5 minutes or until bread crumbs are lightly browned and cheese is melted.

Yield: 6 servings.

Eastern Indian Potatoes
"An Asian-Indian husband shared this favorite recipe."

6 medium potatoes, cut in 1-inch
  cubes
3 tablespoons vegetable oil
1 teaspoon mustard seed
  (preferably black)
1 teaspoon fennel seed (optional)
½ teaspoon cumin seed (optional)
1 onion, halved and thinly sliced
2 teaspoons finely grated
  gingerroot
2 cloves garlic, finely chopped

¼ teaspoon hot cayenne pepper
  (or to taste)
½ teaspoon turmeric
1 teaspoon salt
1½ tablespoons chopped cilantro
  (optional)
1 tablespoon lemon juice
½ cup frozen peas, thawed and
  thoroughly drained
1 tablespoon roasted cashews

Boil potatoes until tender but still firm, using as little water as possible; drain. Assemble and prepare ingredients as listed.

In a heavy 12-inch skillet, heat oil until a drop of water flicked into the oil sizzles instantly. Add mustard seed, fennel seed and cumin seed. Fry until mustard seeds start to pop; cover with a lid so seeds will not pop out of the skillet.

When most of the seeds have popped, add onion. Fry until golden brown, stirring frequently. When brown, add gingerroot and garlic and keep stirring. Fry 5 minutes more.

Add cayenne pepper and turmeric. Fry about 1 minute. Add boiled potatoes. Stir until spices and onion are thoroughly mixed. Add salt and fry about 10 minutes more, until potatoes are dry. Add cilantro, lemon juice and peas.

Cook a few more minutes until peas are hot. Stir in cashews.

This dish is good with most plain meat dishes.

Yield: 4-6 servings.

Undercover Potatoes

"delicious accompaniment for turkey or ham"

6 medium potatoes, peeled and
   thinly sliced
⅓ cup butter
⅓ cup flour
½ teaspoon salt
¼ teaspoon pepper
3 cups milk

2 cups (8 oz.) sharp cheese, diced
1 (2 oz.) jar chopped pimiento,
   drained (optional)
4 green onions, thinly sliced
2 cups soft bread crumbs
⅓ cup butter, melted
Paprika

Cook potatoes in water for 10 minutes; drain.

In small saucepan, melt ⅓ cup butter; blend in flour, salt and pepper. Add milk and cook, stirring constantly, until thick and smooth. Remove from heat. Stir in cheese, pimiento, onions and potatoes. Put in a 1½-quart casserole dish.

Mix bread crumbs and ⅓ cup butter. Cover potato mixture with crumbs. Sprinkle with paprika. Bake at 350 degrees for 30 minutes.

Yield: 8 servings.

Stuffed Baked Potatoes
"baked potatoes dressed up"

3 large baking potatoes
1 cup cottage cheese
2 tablespoons chopped chives
   or onion

2-4 tablespoons butter
1 teaspoon salt
¼ teaspoon pepper
2 tablespoons chopped pimiento

Scrub potatoes and bake at 400 degrees for 1 hour. Cut hot potatoes in half lengthwise, scoop out potato; save shells.

Whip together potato, cottage cheese, chives, butter, salt and pepper until very fluffy. Fold in pimiento. Divide into 6 potato shells. Return to oven for about 12 minutes until potatoes are hot and slightly browned.

May be made in advance and reheated just before serving.

Yield: 6 servings.

Orange-Glazed Sweet Potatoes
"a colorful fall or winter side dish"

6 large canned sweet potatoes,
   halved lengthwise
1 cup orange juice

2 teaspoons grated orange peel
3 tablespoons butter or margarine
⅓ cup packed brown sugar

Place sweet potatoes in 8x8x2-inch baking dish. Combine remaining ingredients in small saucepan and cook until thick. Pour over sweet potatoes. Bake at 350 degrees for 30 minutes.

Yield: 6-8 servings.

Tomatoes Oregano
"best when tomatoes are still in season"

6 large ripe tomatoes, halved
Oregano
Garlic powder
Freshly ground pepper

1 cup soft bread crumbs
1 tablespoon olive oil
¼ cup grated Parmesan cheese

Place tomatoes, cut side up, in 13x9x2-inch baking pan. Sprinkle liberally with seasonings.

In small bowl, mix bread crumbs and olive oil. Top each tomato with crumb mixture and Parmesan cheese. Bake at 350 degrees for 20 minutes.

Yield: 12 servings.

Baked Vegetable Medley
"Strike up the band!"

2 large new red or Idaho potatoes
2 large onions, sliced
3 large carrots, thinly sliced
2 (10 oz.) packages frozen
    chopped spinach, thawed
    and drained
1 (10¾ oz.) can condensed cream
    of celery soup

⅓ cup chopped parsley
⅓ cup milk
1 tablespoon Dijon mustard
¾ teaspoon dried basil
¾ teaspoon oregano
1 cup (4 oz.) shredded
    Cheddar cheese

Scrub new potatoes or peel Idaho potatoes; cut into thin slices.

In well-greased, shallow 3-quart casserole, layer half of the potatoes, onions and carrots. Arrange spinach on top; repeat layers of remaining potatoes, onions and carrots.

Stir together soup, parsley, milk, mustard, basil and oregano. Spoon over vegetables.

Bake at 350 degrees for 1½ hours. Sprinkle cheese evenly over top and bake about 10 minutes longer or until cheese melts.

Yield: 8 servings.

Vegetable Nests
"adds an elegant flair to a roast beef dinner"

1 package frozen patty shells
8 oz. fresh mushrooms, sliced
2 tablespoons butter
1 clove garlic, minced
3 broccoli flowerets, cut in pieces
3 cauliflower flowerets, cut in
    pieces
1 medium zucchini, sliced thin
½ cup sliced green pepper

1 medium carrot, cut into
    julienne strips
½ cup sliced red pepper
    (optional)
½ teaspoon marjoram
1½ cup chicken broth
Salt and pepper to taste
2 tablespoons cornstarch
¼ cup water

Prepare patty shells according to package directions.

Meanwhile, in a large skillet, brown mushrooms in butter with garlic. Add vegetables, marjoram and chicken broth. Bring to a boil; cover and simmer 10 minutes or until vegetables are tender. Add salt and pepper.

Blend cornstarch and water. Add to vegetable mixture. Cook, stirring constantly, until thickened. Serve in baked patty shells.

Yield: 6 side dish or 3 main dish servings.

Zucchini-Corn Casserole

"Vegetarian children and prolific zucchini crops led to this favorite casserole."

3 pounds zucchini, parboiled
  and cubed
1 (16 oz.) can cream-style corn
4 eggs, slightly beaten
1 medium onion, chopped
1 medium green pepper,
  chopped

2 tablespoons butter, melted
1¼ teaspoons salt
Dash of pepper
1 cup (4 oz.) shredded sharp
  Cheddar cheese
Paprika

Combine zucchini, corn and eggs. Sauté onion and green pepper in butter until golden. Add to other vegetables. Add seasonings.

Turn into greased 2-quart casserole. Sprinkle with cheese, then paprika. Bake at 350 degrees for 40 minutes or until lightly browned and bubbly.

Yield: 10-12 servings.

Stir-Fried Country Vegetables

"putsy, but really good"

10 tablespoons vegetable oil
4 large carrots, thinly sliced
1½ teaspoons salt
8 oz. Chinese pea pods or 1 (6 oz.)
  package frozen pea pods,
  thawed
2 cups fresh green beans, halved
16 oz. fresh mushrooms, halved

1 pint cherry tomatoes
1 small bunch broccoli, cut into
  2x1-inch pieces
1 small head cauliflower,
  separated into flowerets
1 medium onion, quartered
½ cup water
2 tablespoons soy sauce

Heat 2 tablespoons oil in 8-quart Dutch oven over medium high heat. Add carrots and ¼ teaspoon salt and cook until carrots are tender-crisp, about 3-5 minutes, stirring often. With slotted spoon, remove to large bowl.

In 1 tablespoon hot oil, cook and stir pea pods 1-2 minutes. Remove to bowl.

In 1 tablespoon oil plus ¼ teaspoon salt, cook green beans until tender-crisp. Remove to bowl.

In 3 tablespoons hot oil, stir mushrooms and ½ teaspoon salt until mushrooms are coated. Cover; cook 3-5 minutes, stirring occasionally. Remove to bowl.

In 1 tablespoon hot oil, cook and stir tomatoes until heated through, about 1 minute. Remove to bowl.

In 2 tablespoons hot oil, stir broccoli, cauliflower and onion until well coated; add water and ½ teaspoon salt; cover and cook 5-10 minutes until tender-crisp, stirring occasionally.

Return all vegetables to Dutch oven; add soy sauce; mix well. Spoon vegetables onto platter. Serve hot, or cover and refrigerate to serve cold later.

Yield: 8-10 servings.

Mixed Vegetables with Almonds
"easy and different"

1 (16 oz.) package frozen cauliflower
1 (16 oz.) package frozen green beans
1 (16 oz.) package frozen peas
½ cup milk

1 (10¾ oz.) can condensed cream of chicken soup
1½ cups (6 oz.) shredded Cheddar cheese
1 (2 oz.) jar diced pimiento, drained
½ cup slivered almonds

Cook vegetables until half done. Add milk to soup, stir until smooth. Add cheese and pimiento, then combine with vegetables.

Place in greased 3-quart casserole. Sprinkle with almonds. Bake at 350 degrees for 30 minutes.

May be made ahead and refrigerated; increase baking time to 45-60 minutes.

Yield: 8-10 servings.

Spaghetti Squash with Green Beans
"harvest hospitality fare"

4 cups cooked spaghetti squash (about 1 large squash)
1 cup whole kernel corn
¼ cup margarine, melted
½ cup fine dry bread crumbs
4 eggs, slightly beaten

1 cup evaporated milk
2 cups (8 oz.) shredded Monterey Jack cheese
1 teaspoon salt
Pepper to taste
1 pound French-style green beans

Combine all ingredients except green beans. Mix lightly and thoroughly. Pour into well-greased 8-cup ring mold and place in larger pan with about 1 inch of hot water. Bake at 350 degrees for 40-45 minutes.

Cook green beans. Cool mold slightly before unmolding onto platter. Place hot green beans in center of mold.

Yield: 8-10 servings.

Harvest Vegetable Casserole
"colorful"

1 (11 oz.) package frozen white
  and wild rice
1 (10 oz.) package baby lima
  beans, frozen in butter sauce
1 medium onion, sliced
1 green pepper, cut in thin
  2-inch strips

1 cup sliced celery
3 tablespoons vegetable oil
1 (15 oz.) can kidney beans,
  drained
2 medium tomatoes, chopped
1 teaspoon basil

Cook rice and lima beans according to package directions.

Meanwhile, in large skillet, sauté onion, green pepper and celery in oil until tender-crisp. Add rice, lima beans, kidney beans, tomatoes and basil. Heat thoroughly.

Yield: 6-8 servings.

Zucchini or Eggplant Parmesan
"tastes and looks like lasagne"

2 eggs
1½ cups ricotta or cottage cheese
1 large or 6 small zucchini or 1
  large eggplant, sliced
Tomato Sauce (below)

2 cups (8 oz.) mozzarella cheese,
  shredded
½ cup grated Parmesan cheese
1 cup bread crumbs

Mix eggs with ricotta cheese. In oiled 13x9x2-inch pan, layer zucchini, cheese and egg mixture, tomato sauce and mozzarella cheese. Sprinkle with Parmesan cheese, then bread crumbs.

Bake at 350 degrees for 30 minutes or until bubbly. Let stand 10-15 minutes before slicing.

Yield: 6-8 servings.

Tomato Sauce:

2 cloves garlic, mashed
1 medium onion, chopped
1 tablespoon olive or
  vegetable oil
½ teaspoon salt
¼ teaspoon pepper
1 (8 oz.) can tomato purée
  or sauce

1 (6 oz.) can tomato paste
1 (6 oz.) can water
1 (6 oz.) can dry red wine
½ teaspoon each dried basil and
  oregano or 1 teaspoon Italian
  herb mix

Brown garlic and onion in oil. Add remaining ingredients; simmer a few minutes until thickened.

Yield: about 2⅔ cups.

MEATS
& FISH ☑

The Judge's Favorite Pot Roast

"Apples and sauerkraut distinguish this dish."

2-pound beef arm or chuck roast
3 tablespoons margarine
Salt and pepper to taste
Onion powder to taste
Garlic powder to taste
½ cup red wine

½ cup water
2 large or 3 medium potatoes, coarsely shredded
3 apples, peeled, cored and sliced
1 (16 oz.) can sauerkraut, drained

In large skillet with tight cover, brown roast on all sides in margarine. Season with salt, pepper, onion and garlic. Mix red wine with water; pour over meat. Immediately cover and reduce heat. Cook 2-3 hours.

Thirty minutes before serving, push meat to side and put potatoes in the juices to prevent discoloring. Add apple slices and sauerkraut on top. Cover and cook ½ hour. Serve with horseradish, if desired.

Yield: 4 servings.

Sauerbraten

"a 4-star recipe"

1 quart water, boiled and cooled
1¼ cups cider vinegar
2 onions, sliced
2 tablespoons sugar
2 bay leaves
10 peppercorns
1 tablespoon mustard seed
½ teaspoon nutmeg
1½ teaspoons salt
3-pound beef chuck
    or eye of round roast

3 tablespoons vegetable oil
2 cups water
1 teaspoon salt
1 bay leaf
2 teaspoons paprika
½ teaspoon nutmeg
1 (13 oz.) can evaporated milk
3 tablespoons flour
1 (¾-1 oz.) envelope
    beef gravy mix

Mix water, vinegar, onions, sugar, 2 bay leaves, peppercorns, mustard seed, nutmeg and 1½ teaspoons salt together for marinade. Place meat in bowl and pour marinade over it. Marinate in refrigerator for at least 36 hours, turning occasionally.

Remove roast from marinade and drain, reserving the marinade. In large heavy kettle, brown meat on all sides in hot oil. Remove onions from marinade and add to kettle with 2 cups of marinade and 2 cups water. Add 1 teaspoon salt, 1 bay leaf, paprika and nutmeg. Cover and simmer 3 hours.

Remove roast from kettle and keep warm. Mix evaporated milk with flour and beef gravy mix; add to hot meat juices. Bring to a boil, stirring constantly and cook 1-2 minutes. Gravy will be thin.

Serve sauerbraten with red cabbage, potato pancakes and gravy.

Recipe makes a large quantity of thin gravy which may be frozen.

Yield: 6 servings.

Banner and Bands Beef
"makes a grand entrance"

¼ cup olive oil
3½-4 pounds lean stewing beef, cut into 1½-inch cubes
¼ cup sweet vermouth or sherry
¼ cup butter or margarine
1 (¼-inch thick) slice lean ham, diced
24 small white onions, peeled
16 oz. small fresh mushrooms
3 cloves garlic, minced

2 tablespoons tomato paste
¼ cup soy sauce
6 tablespoons flour
2 (10½ oz.) cans beef broth
2½ cups red Burgundy
¼ teaspoon pepper
2 bay leaves
½ teaspoon thyme
½ cup fresh parsley, chopped

Heat oil in skillet. Brown beef a little at a time. Transfer beef to 4-quart casserole; sprinkle with vermouth. Melt butter in same skillet. Add and quickly brown ham, onions, mushrooms and garlic.

Transfer to the casserole using a slotted spoon. Add tomato paste, soy sauce and flour to pan drippings in skillet. Slowly add beef broth; bring to a boil, stirring constantly. Cook for 1 minute. Stir in ½ cup of wine and pepper. Pour sauce over beef. Add bay leaves and thyme.

Bake covered at 350 degrees until meat is tender, 3-4 hours, adding remaining wine from time to time.

Garnish with parsley. Serve over rice or noodles.

Casserole can be prepared a day ahead and refrigerated or frozen. To serve, skim off any fat. Reheat, covered, at 350 degrees for 1 hour.

Yield: 8-10 servings.

Amazing Grace Stew
"at home in the range"

1½-2 pounds lean beef stew meat, cut in 1-inch cubes
1 medium onion, diced or sliced
6 stalks celery, cut in large diagonal pieces
4-6 carrots, cut in large chunks
1 large potato, cut in chunks
1 green pepper, cut in large chunks or strips (optional)
⅓ cup red wine

1 (16 oz.) can stewed tomatoes
1 teaspoon salt
1 teaspoon sugar
2 tablespoons minute tapioca
1 teaspoon Spice Islands Fines Herbes
Freshly ground pepper to taste
1 (16 oz.) can whole onions, drained
Snipped parsley

Place meat and vegetables in large roaster. Add remaining ingredients except onions and parsley. Mix and cover roaster. Bake at 250 degrees for 5 hours. During last hour, add onions.

Serve from a tureen, garnished with parsley.

Yield: 4-6 servings.

Beef Brisket with Barbecue Sauce
"great for a football weekend"

5-6 pound beef brisket
Garlic salt
Celery salt

Onion salt
Liquid smoke or teriyaki sauce
Barbecue Sauce (below)

Remove fat from brisket. Sprinkle brisket generously with garlic, celery and onion salts. Sprinkle with liquid smoke. Put in pan, cover with foil and marinate overnight in refrigerator.

Roast at 275 degrees for 1 hour per pound. Refrigerate to cool.

Remove fat from liquid and thinly slice meat. Pour Barbecue Sauce over meat; cover pan. Bake at 300 degrees for 1 hour.

Yield: 12-15 servings.

Barbecue Sauce:

2 tablespoons packed brown sugar
2 tablespoons vinegar
2 teaspoons Worcestershire sauce

½ cup catsup
2 teaspoons dry mustard
½ teaspoon salt
5 drops Tabasco sauce

Combine all ingredients.

Yield: about ¾ cup.

Barbecued Beef

"A do-ahead teen pleaser."

5-7 pound bottom round beef
    roast
1 (14 oz.) bottle catsup
1 (14 oz.) bottle water
1 (14 oz.) bottle vinegar
1 (8 oz.) can tomato sauce
½ teaspoon garlic powder

2 teaspoons salt
½ teaspoon pepper
1 teaspoon curry powder
¾ cup granulated sugar
½ cup packed brown sugar
2 teaspoons liquid smoke

Roast beef to medium or medium rare. When cool, cut in thin slices. Place sliced meat in a 13x9x2-inch pan or 3-quart casserole dish.

In large saucepan, combine remaining ingredients; simmer for 5 minutes. Pour sauce over meat. Refrigerate for a few hours or overnight.

Before serving, simmer for 20 minutes or heat in oven at 325 degrees for 30 minutes.

Yield: 10-12 servings.

Braised Brisket of Beef

"This is an authentic Jewish pot roast, with a very special flavor.
A real family favorite."

4-7 pound beef brisket, excess
    fat trimmed
1 teaspoon salt
Freshly ground black pepper

Garlic powder
Paprika
1 large onion, coarsely chopped
Bay leaf

Heat oven to 475 degrees. Wipe meat carefully with damp paper towel and season liberally with salt, pepper, garlic powder and paprika. Place brisket in large roasting pan with cover.

Brown meat in oven, turning once or twice. Stir in chopped onion and bay leaf. Baste with pan juices, adding very little water. Cover and reduce oven temperature to 325 degrees. Bake until fork-tender, turning meat 2-3 times.

Raw vegetables of choice may be added during last hour. Baste these also with pan juices.

Allow meat to rest a few minutes. Slice across grain of meat.

Yield: 8-10 servings.

Sirloin with Vegetables
"stir-frying can't be any easier"

¾ pound sirloin steak, cut into
    1-inch strips
2 tablespoons vegetable oil
¼ cup minced onion
4 oz. fresh mushrooms, sliced
½ cup sliced green pepper

1 cup sliced celery
2 tablespoons chopped pimiento
1 cup fresh or frozen green beans
1 tablespoon cornstarch
¼ cup soy sauce
¾ cup water

In a heavy skillet or wok, brown sirloin in 1 tablespoon oil. Remove meat. Sauté onion and mushrooms in 1 tablespoon oil.

Add green pepper, celery, pimiento and green beans. Stir-fry until vegetables are crisp-tender, 4-5 minutes.

Mix cornstarch with soy sauce and water. Add to vegetables. Bring to a boil, stirring constantly. Return meat to skillet and heat through.

Serve with rice.

Yield: 4 servings.

Beef and Pea Pods
"a stir-fry favorite"

3 tablespoons sherry
2 tablespoons Kikkoman
    soy sauce
1 teaspoon sugar
½ teaspoon ginger
1 clove garlic, minced
1½ pounds boneless beef sirloin,
    thinly sliced
3 beef bouillon cubes

1 cup hot water
3 tablespoons peanut oil
6 oz. Chinese pea pods
2 cups sliced fresh mushrooms
1 cup sliced green onions
1 cup sliced water chestnuts
1 cup fresh bean sprouts
3 tablespoons cornstarch

Combine sherry, soy sauce, sugar, ginger and garlic; mix with meat. Refrigerate 3-4 hours.

Just before stir-frying, mix beef bouillon cubes with hot water. Drain meat and reserve marinade.

Heat peanut oil in a wok or skillet to high heat. Stir-fry meat until grey. Add peas, mushrooms and marinade; stir-fry 1 minute.

Add onions, water chestnuts and bean sprouts; stir-fry 1 minute more. Mix cornstarch with bouillon and water; add to wok, stirring constantly. Bring to a boil and boil 1 minute. Serve over rice.

Yield: 6 servings.

Fantastic Swiss Steak
"very attractive, very tasty"

2 pounds beef round steak
1 clove garlic
½ teaspoon salt
¼ teaspoon pepper
½ cup flour
¼ cup margarine

½ cup chopped onion
1 cup chopped carrots
1 cup chopped green pepper
1 cup chopped celery
1 (16 oz.) can tomatoes
1 cup beef bouillon

Rub steak with garlic. Pound in salt, pepper and as much flour as meat will hold. Cut steak into serving-size pieces.

Melt margarine in Dutch oven. Sear both sides of meat; add vegetables and bouillon. Cover and bake at 325 degrees for 2 hours. Serve with noodles.

Yield: 4-6 servings.

Gretchen's Gourmet Salisbury Steak
"First Family favorite"

2 pounds lean ground beef
1 (4 oz.) can mushrooms, drained
   and chopped
1 cup dairy sour cream
¾ cup bread crumbs

1 teaspoon chives or
   dried onion flakes
1 teaspoon salt
¼ teaspoon pepper
Garlic salt to taste

Combine all ingredients; mix well. Form into 8 patties. Broil.

Yield: 8 servings.

Teriyaki
"will guarantee good international relations"

1 teaspoon grated gingerroot
2 cloves garlic, minced
½ cup Kikkoman soy sauce

¼ cup sherry or sauterne
¼ cup sugar
2 pounds beef sirloin tip roast

Mix gingerroot, garlic, soy sauce, wine and sugar until sugar is dissolved. Slice beef about ¼-inch thick. Pour marinade over beef pieces and refrigerate 2-3 hours, turning pieces once.

Broil beef pieces 5 minutes per side. Meat will have a nice glaze.

Yield: 6 servings.

Ossi Buchi
"stew Italian-style"

3 pounds veal shins or center cut
  beef shanks, cut into 1-inch
  pieces
½ cup flour
2 tablespoons vegetable oil
2 tablespoons butter
2 teaspoons salt
½ teaspoon pepper
¼ teaspoon rosemary
¾ cup chopped onion

¼ cup shredded carrots
1 stalk celery, chopped
1 cup dry white wine
1 tablespoon tomato paste
½ cup water
2 tablespoons grated lemon peel
1 clove garlic, minced
2 tablespoons minced fresh
  parsley

Coat meat with flour. Brown in 5-quart Dutch oven or large kettle in oil and butter. Add salt, pepper, rosemary, onion, carrots and celery. Cook for 5 minutes. Add wine, tomato paste and water; cover and simmer for 2 hours.

Add lemon peel, garlic and parsley; cook for 5 minutes. Serve with rice.

Yield: 6-8 servings.

Beef Under Wraps
"One is a substantial serving."

10 crepes (below)
¾ pound lean ground beef
1 small onion, finely chopped
1 (4 oz.) can mushrooms, drained
½ teaspoon salt
¼ teaspoon pepper
1 teaspoon dry mustard
2 cloves garlic, minced (optional)
½ cup catsup
1 tablespoon steak sauce
1 teaspoon oregano

1 teaspoon parsley
1 teaspoon rosemary
2 cups (8 oz.) shredded Cheddar
  cheese
½ cup grated Parmesan cheese
½ cup dry sherry
½ cup grated Parmesan cheese
20 thin slices mozzarella cheese
1 teaspoon paprika
2 tablespoons butter, melted

Prepare crepes.

Brown ground beef, onion, and mushrooms; drain. Add salt, pepper, mustard and garlic; simmer 5 minutes. Add catsup and steak sauce.

Combine herbs, Cheddar cheese and ½ cup Parmesan cheese. Add to meat mixture. Cover; simmer until cheese is half melted.

Remove from heat. Spread beef mixture on crepes and roll up, securing with toothpicks. Place in greased baking dish. Sprinkle with

Stuffed Beef Roll-ups

"pleasing appearance, easy to make"

1 (6½ oz.) package
   stuffing-with-rice mix
1 pound beef round tip steak (ask
   butcher to make 8 thin slices)

1 (10½ oz.) can French
   onion soup
½ soup can water

Prepare stuffing mix according to package directions.

To make individual roll-ups, place 2 tablespoonfuls of stuffing on each beef slice. Roll up and place seam side down in a 9x9x2-inch baking dish. Extra stuffing can be spooned into the dish.

Combine French onion soup and water; pour evenly over roll-ups. Cover with foil. Bake at 350 degrees for 1½ hours.

Yield: 4 servings.

Wild Rice Pizza

"a majority leader"

2 cups wild rice
3 tablespoons butter or margarine
2-3 green peppers, cut in strips
3 chicken bouillon cubes
3 cups boiling water
1-1½ pounds lean ground beef
1 cup chopped onion
1 cup chopped celery
1 clove garlic, minced

3 cups tomato sauce
1 teaspoon crushed oregano
   leaves
¼ teaspoon pepper
1 cup (4 oz.) shredded Cheddar
   cheese
1 cup (4 oz.) shredded farmer
   or mozzarella cheese

Rinse and drain rice; cook in melted butter in large skillet on medium high heat until lightly toasted, stirring frequently, about 10-12 minutes. Spread rice in 13x9x2-inch baking pan. Arrange green pepper on top.

Dissolve bouillon cubes in boiling water; pour over rice mixture. Cover tightly with aluminum foil. Bake at 375 degrees for 35 minutes.

Meanwhile, cook meat, onion, celery and garlic in skillet until meat is browned. Stir in tomato sauce and spices. Simmer, covered, for 5 minutes. Pour over peppers and rice. Cover and continue baking 15 minutes longer.

Sprinkle with cheeses and bake uncovered 10 minutes or until cheese is bubbly.

Yield: 8-10 servings.

Variation: Brown rice may be substituted for half the wild rice.

No-Veto Kids' Casserole

"this gets the kids' votes"

8 oz. uncooked spaghetti
2 tablespoons butter
⅓ cup grated Parmesan cheese
2 eggs, well beaten
1 pound ground beef
½ cup chopped onion
1 (8 oz.) can tomatoes, chopped

1 (6 oz.) can tomato paste
1 teaspoon oregano
1 teaspoon garlic salt
1 cup cottage cheese
1 cup (4 oz.) shredded
  mozzarella cheese

Cook spaghetti; drain and stir in butter. Add Parmesan cheese and eggs; mix well. Line bottom of 10-inch pie pan with this mixture.

Brown beef and onion; drain off excess fat. Stir undrained tomatoes, tomato paste, oregano and garlic salt into meat. Heat through.

Spread cottage cheese over spaghetti, then spread beef and tomato mixture over cheese. Bake uncovered at 350 degrees for 20 minutes.

Sprinkle with mozzarella cheese; bake 5 minutes more.

Yield: 8 servings.

Zucchini-Beef Casserole

"greet the zucchini season with a new dish"

1 tablespoon vegetable oil
1 cup finely chopped onion
3 medium unpeeled zucchini,
  cubed
2 cloves garlic, minced
1 pound ground beef
2 eggs, slightly beaten
1 cup fresh French bread crumbs

6 tablespoons grated
  Parmesan cheese
¾ teaspoon dried oregano,
  crumbled
1½ teaspoons salt
¼ teaspoon pepper
2 cups tomato sauce
2 tablespoons grated
  Parmesan cheese

Heat oil in heavy 10-inch skillet; add onion and cook over moderate heat until tender, 8-10 minutes. Add zucchini and garlic; cook 8 minutes, stirring frequently. Drain and put in large mixing bowl.

Brown ground beef over moderate heat. Drain off excess fat. Add meat to vegetables with eggs, bread crumbs, 6 tablespoons Parmesan cheese, oregano, salt and pepper.

In 9x9x2-inch baking dish, spread ½ cup tomato sauce. Pour meat mixture into dish. Pour remaining tomato sauce over meat. Sprinkle on 2 tablespoons Parmesan cheese. Bake uncovered at 375 degrees for 30 minutes.

Yield: 4-6 servings.

Mexican Chimi Chongas

"This is one of our favorite meals! It looks overwhelming on paper,
but the proof is in the eating."

16 (10-inch) flour tortillas (fresh,
  found in dairy case)
Vegetable oil
Chili-Beef Filling (below)
10 cups (2½ pounds) shredded
  Cheddar cheese
8 cups shredded iceberg lettuce

Green Chili Salsa (below)
1 pound dairy sour cream
Guacamole (see index)
Chopped green onions
Chopped ripe olives

Soften tortillas, one at a time, in large skillet with a little oil. Warm both sides until they have golden spots on them. Drain between layers of paper towels.

Put about ¼ cup of Chili-Beef Filling in center of each tortilla. Sprinkle about 2 tablespoons cheese on top. Fold in two ends and roll up.

Fry chimis in oil, turning once when they are light brown and crisp.

Place each chimi on a serving plate; top with about ½ cup shredded cheese, ½ cup shredded lettuce, 2 tablespoons Green Chili Salsa, a dollop of sour cream, Guacamole, green onions and olives.

Chimi Chongas are very filling — serve only one per person. With a fresh fruit salad and a light dessert, they make a good company meal.

Yield: 16 servings.

Chili-Beef Filling:

Vegetable oil
3-pound beef chuck roast
½ teaspoon garlic salt
¼ teaspoon pepper
Beef bouillon cubes
2 tablespoons oil
Water
1 medium onion, chopped

1 (14 oz.) can stewed tomatoes,
  chopped
1 teaspoon garlic salt
1 tablespoon cumin
1 tablespoon crushed oregano
  leaves
1 (4 oz.) can chopped green
  chilies, drained

Put oil in Dutch oven and brown roast on both sides. Cover roast with water (for every cup of water used, add 1 beef bouillon cube). Add garlic salt and pepper; simmer covered for 2½ to 3 hours or until meat falls apart.

Remove meat from liquid; let cool. Reserve liquid. Shred meat. Refrigerate. Discard fat from liquid.

Put shredded meat in Dutch oven; add remaining ingredients except chilies. Add some of reserved meat juice, beginning with ½ cup so it will not be runny.

Simmer 30 minutes. Add chiles. Mixture may be frozen or refrigerated until ready to use in Chimi Chongas.

Can be used as filling for many Mexican dishes such as enchiladas and burritos.

Yield: 16 servings.

Green Chili Salsa:

2 (28 oz.) cans tomatoes, chopped, or 4-6 large fresh tomatoes, chopped
1 large onion, chopped
4-5 stalks celery, chopped
½ teaspoon garlic salt

½ teaspoon oregano leaves
½ teaspoon cumin
½ teaspoon parsley flakes
1 (4 oz.) can chopped green chilies, drained

Combine all ingredients; refrigerate overnight.

Yield: about 9 cups.

Lobbyist's Lasagne
"very firm and spicy"

1 pound ground beef
1 pound spicy pork sausage
3 (8 oz.) cans tomato sauce
2 (10¾ oz.) cans tomato soup
1½ tablespoons Italian seasoning

1 pound uncooked lasagne noodles
2 cups (8 oz.) shredded Cheddar cheese
3 cups (8 oz.) shredded mozzarella cheese

In skillet, brown beef and sausage together; drain off excess fat. Add tomato sauce, tomato soup and seasoning. Cook until sauce and soup are hot.

Spread small amount of meat and sauce in bottom of 13x9x2-inch baking pan. Place layer of uncooked noodles on top of sauce, then a layer of meat and sauce, then a layer of cheese. Repeat layering process, ending with a heavy layer of meat sauce and cheese. Cover noodles with sauce so they will not dry out during baking.

Cover and refrigerate for at least 24 hours. Bake uncovered at 350 degrees for 45-55 minutes.

May be frozen. Thaw completely before baking.

Yield: 10-12 servings.

Supper Nachos

"Easy! I have made this for 50 people."

1½ pounds ground beef
1 medium onion, chopped
½ teaspoon salt
1 (4 oz.) can chopped green
   chilies, drained
1 (16 oz.) can refried beans
3½ cups (14 oz.) shredded
   Cheddar cheese (can be half
   Monterey Jack cheese)

¾ cup green chili salsa
1 cup dairy sour cream
½ cup chopped green onions
½ cup chopped ripe olives
1 large or 2 small avocados,
   cut in thin wedges
Round taco chips

Brown ground beef and onion; drain off excess fat. Stir in salt and chilies. Layer in 8x8x2-inch pan in the following order: refried beans, ground beef mixture, shredded cheese, green chili salsa.

Bake at 375 degrees for 20 minutes or until cheese is melted. Garnish with sour cream, green onions, olives and avocados. Insert taco chips around the edge of the casserole in an upright fashion. Serve with extra taco chips on the side.

Yield: 6-8 servings.

Beef and Eggplant Casserole

"cheers from the gallery"

1 large eggplant
2 cups uncooked macaroni
1½ pounds ground beef
1 onion, chopped
2 tomatoes, chopped
¼ cup catsup
2 teaspoons salt

1½ teaspoons curry powder
¼ teaspoon pepper
½ teaspoon ginger
¼ teaspoon cumin
Rich White Sauce (next page)
½ cup (2 oz.) shredded
   Cheddar cheese

Slice eggplant and parboil in 2 quarts boiling water. Cook macaroni in eggplant water until almost done.

Brown ground beef and onion together in large skillet; drain off excess fat. Add tomatoes, catsup and spices.

Cut up eggplant and add to macaroni; mix well. Pour into 13x9x2-inch baking pan. Layer meat mixture on macaroni; cover with Rich White Sauce; sprinkle with cheese. Bake uncovered at 350 degrees for 30 minutes.

Yield: 12 servings.

Rich White Sauce:

6 tablespoons margarine
⅓ cup flour
1 teaspoon dry mustard

3 eggs, slightly beaten
2½ cups milk

Melt margarine in saucepan. Add flour and cook until bubbly; blend in mustard. Remove from heat. Mix egg and milk together and gradually add to flour mixture. Cook, stirring until thick.

Yield: about 3 cups.

Best Spaghetti Sauce Ever
"slow cooked for a rich flavor"

2 (29 oz.) cans whole tomatoes
   or 16 fresh tomatoes, peeled
2 tablespoons sugar
½ teaspoon salt
1 teaspoon pepper
3 (6 oz.) cans tomato paste
3 cups water
1 teaspoon Italian seasoning
2 eggs, slightly beaten
½ cup milk

4 slices fresh bread, torn into
   pieces
2 pounds lean ground beef
½ cup grated Parmesan cheese
½ cup chopped onion
½ teaspoon salt
2 teaspoons pepper
1 tablespoon olive oil
2 cloves garlic, minced
¾ cup grated Parmesan cheese

Mash tomatoes in large kettle. Bring to a boil; add sugar, salt and pepper. Reduce heat and simmer 1 hour until thickened.

Add tomato paste, water and Italian seasoning; simmer 1½ hours.

Mix eggs and milk in a large bowl; add bread and allow to soak for several minutes. Add ground beef, ½ cup Parmesan cheese, onion, salt and pepper. Mix thoroughly.

Sauté garlic in olive oil in large skillet. Add meat mixture to skillet. Pat meat down, forming a large "pancake" that covers the bottom of the skillet. Brown over medium low heat; do not stir. Turn meat and brown other side. After browning is complete, crumble meat.

Add ¾ cup Parmesan cheese and crumbled meat mixture to sauce that has simmered a total of 2½ hours. Simmer another hour.

Yield: 8-10 servings.

Pork Chops and Zucchini Parmesan

"zucchini artfully enhanced or hidden, depending on your viewpoint"

3 tablespoons flour
1½ tablespoons grated
  Parmesan cheese
1 teaspoon salt
½ teaspoon dill weed
¼ teaspoon pepper
1 tablespoon vegetable oil
6 lean pork chops

2 medium onions, sliced
⅓ cup water
3 zucchini, sliced
3 tablespoons grated
  Parmesan cheese
½ teaspoon paprika
Tomato slices
Fresh parsley

Put flour, 1½ tablespoons Parmesan cheese, salt, dill weed and pepper into a paper or plastic bag; shake pork chops in bag.

In electric skillet, heat oil to 350 degrees. Brown chops in oil; place onions over chops. Add water, cover and simmer on low for 15 minutes.

Add zucchini to skillet. Combine leftover flour mixture, 3 tablespoons Parmesan cheese and paprika; sprinkle over zucchini. Do not stir. Cover and simmer for 25 minutes.

Spoon carefully onto platter rimmed with tomato slices and parsley. Serve with rice or noodles.

Yield: 6 servings.

Sarma

(Stuffed Cabbage Leaves)

"a Croatian favorite from the Governor's Residence"

1 medium head cabbage
1 large onion, finely chopped
1 tablespoon vegetable oil
1½ pounds ground pork
1 pound ground ham
½ pound ground beef

1 cup uncooked rice
Salt and pepper
1 egg
1 quart sauerkraut
1 (10¾ oz.) can condensed
  tomato soup (optional)

Core cabbage and place in boiling water until leaves soften; drain and separate leaves.

Sauté onion lightly in oil. Mix with meat, rice, seasoning and egg. Roll generous portions of meat mixture in each leaf. When leaves are all used, shape remaining meat into balls.

Cover bottom of large roasting pan with sauerkraut. Alternate layers of cabbage rolls and meat balls with layers of sauerkraut, ending with layer of sauerkraut on top. Add tomato soup. Nearly cover with cold

water (about 7 cups).
Bring to a boil and simmer about 2 hours. Sarmas can also be baked, using only 3½ cups water, at 350 degrees for 2 hours.

Yield: About 22 sarmas.

Pork Chops and Wild Rice
"primarily a party dish"

1 (8 oz.) package wild rice (1½ cups)	Butter or vegetable oil
1½ quarts water	1 cup minced onion
1½ teaspoons salt	2 (10¾ oz.) cans condensed cream of mushroom soup
8-10 (1-1½-inch thick) lean pork chops	1 cup water
Salt and pepper	3 tablespoons sherry or sauterne

Cook wild rice in 1½ quarts salted water until rice partially opens (about 15 minutes); drain. Place rice in large casserole or 13x9x2-inch baking pan.
Sprinkle pork chops with salt and pepper; brown in butter in heavy skillet. Place chops on top of rice.
In same skillet, sauté onion until golden; drain off fat. Add mushroom soup, 1 cup water and sherry. Bring to a boil, stirring up browned portions for added flavor. Pour over chops and rice.
Cover and bake at 325 degrees for 1-1½ hours until tender.

Yield: 8-10 servings.

Barbecued Spareribs
"bake in a teflon-lined roaster for easy clean-up"

1 onion, finely chopped	3 tablespoons Worcestershire sauce
2 tablespoons vinegar	
2 tablespoons brown sugar	½ tablespoon mustard
2 tablespoons lemon juice	½ tablespoon hot water
1 cup catsup	3 pounds spareribs

Combine all ingredients except ribs in a saucepan. Heat sauce through.
Place ribs in roaster; pour sauce over ribs. Cover and bake at 375 degrees about 2 hours or until ribs are well done.

Yield: 4 servings.

Populist Pork Tenderloin
"simple and appealing"

12 slices bacon
6 pork tenderloins (ask butcher to
  make individual patties)

6 (½-inch) slices tomato
6 (½-inch) slices onion

Cross 2 slices of bacon. Place 1 pork tenderloin on center. Season if desired. Place 1 tomato slice and 1 onion slice on top of meat. Bring bacon ends up and over onion slice; fasten with wooden toothpick. Repeat with remaining ingredients. Place in baking pan and cover.
  Bake at 350 degrees for 30 minutes. Remove cover and bake 30 minutes longer.

Yield: 6 servings.

Microwave Sweet and Sour Pork
"tradition turned hi-tech"

1½ pounds cubed pork
2 tablespoons cornstarch
1 (15¼ oz.) can chunk pineapple
1 small onion, chopped
3 tablespoons soy sauce
¼ cup packed brown sugar

¼ cup vinegar
1 teaspoon salt
¼ teaspoon ginger
1 medium green pepper,
  chopped

Put all ingredients except green pepper in bowl. Stir and cover. Bake on "high" for 25 minutes, stirring occasionally.
  Add green pepper, stir and bake on "high" for 5 minutes. Let stand 10 minutes. Serve over rice.

Yield: 4-6 servings.

Pork Barrel Chops
"stuffed to everybody's liking"

½ package herb stuffing mix
4 thick pork chops

2 cups applesauce
Marjoram, onion powder, garlic
  powder and oregano to taste

Prepare stuffing mix as directed on package.
  With a sharp knife, make an incision to the bone of pork chops to form pocket. Fill pockets with stuffing and place pork chops in baking pan. Bake at 350 degrees for 1 hour.
  Combine applesauce and seasonings; pour over pork chops. Cover and bake an additional hour.

Yield: 4 servings.

Glazed Ham Loaves with Mustard Ring

"This dish is an inexpensive way to serve a crowd."

1 pound smoked ham	½ cup vinegar
1½ pounds lean pork	½ cup water
2 eggs	1½ cups packed brown sugar
1 cup milk	1 tablespoon dry mustard
1 cup fine bread crumbs	Mustard Ring (below)
Pepper to taste	

Have butcher grind ham and pork. Mix with egg, milk, bread crumbs and pepper; form into 12 equal oval-shaped loaves. Place in 13x9x2-inch baking dish.

Heat vinegar, water, brown sugar and dry mustard together and pour over loaves. Bake at 350 degrees for 1 hour. Turn the loaves after 30 minutes to give a nice glaze overall. Serve with Mustard Ring.

Loaves freeze well before or after baking.

Yield: 12 small oval loaves.

Mustard Ring:

4 eggs, beaten	¾ cup vinegar
¾ cup sugar	Salt and white pepper (optional)
2½ teaspoons dry mustard	2 envelopes unflavored gelatin
Horseradish to taste	½ cup water
¼ cup water	1 pint whipping cream, whipped

Combine eggs, sugar, dry mustard, horseradish, ¼ cup water, vinegar, salt and pepper in top of double boiler. Cook over simmering water until mixture is smooth and thick and coats a metal spoon.

Soften gelatin in ½ cup water; add to custard mixture and mix thoroughly. Cool to lukewarm. Fold in whipped cream.

Pour into 6-cup ring mold. Refrigerate until firm.

Yield: 20 servings.

Alsatian Casserole
"pork chops, potatoes and onions blend in a slow oven"

6 slices lean bacon
4 (1-inch thick) loin pork chops
4 large boiling potatoes, peeled
  and thinly sliced
2 medium onions, thinly sliced
½ teaspoon salt
¼ teaspoon pepper

¼ teaspoon caraway seed
¾-1 cup dry white wine or
  bouillon
2 cloves garlic, lightly crushed
1 tablespoon chopped fresh
  parsley

Fry 2 slices bacon until crisp; drain and crumble. Set aside.
Trim fat from pork chops; brown chops in bacon drippings.
Layer half the potatoes in 5-quart Dutch oven; top with half the
onion slices and half the salt and pepper. Place chops in a single layer
on top of the onions. Layer remaining potatoes, onions, salt and
pepper on top of pork. Crush caraway seed and add with wine and
garlic. Place 4 slices uncooked bacon on top.
Cover casserole with a double thickness of aluminum foil and the
Dutch oven lid. Bake at 300 degrees for 2½ hours.
Discard the bacon strips; drain off fat and garnish with crumbled
bacon and parsley.

Serve with a sweet and sour sauerkraut salad, good dark rye bread and ice cold
beer.

Yield: 4 servings.

Sherried Chicken
"won on the first ballot"

½ cup flour
2 teaspoons salt
3-pound frying chicken, cut up
¼ cup margarine
½ cup sherry

2 tablespoons soy sauce
2 tablespoons lemon juice
¼ cup finely chopped preserved
  ginger
¼ cup margarine

Combine flour and salt; coat chicken pieces. Brown chicken in ¼ cup
margarine in large skillet. Place chicken in 2-quart covered baking dish.
In skillet, combine remaining ingredients. Bring to a boil and pour
over chicken. Cover and bake at 350 degrees for about 1 hour. Turn
once during baking.

Yield: 4 servings.

Mexican Chicken

"flavor of this unusual chicken dish improves upon reheating"

½ cup flour
1 teaspoon salt
½ teaspoon pepper
2 tablespoons chili powder
¼ teaspoon oregano leaves
4-5 pound chicken, cut into
   serving pieces, skin removed

¼ cup margarine
¼ cup vegetable oil
½ cup sliced stuffed olives
1 cup sliced onions
1 cup water
½ cup chopped walnuts

Mix flour and spices in small paper or plastic bag; coat chicken pieces by shaking in bag. Place chicken in large covered casserole or 13x9x2-inch baking dish.

Melt margarine and oil together and pour over chicken. Cover and bake at 350 degrees for 1 hour.

Remove from oven and cover chicken with olives and onions; pour on water. Cover and bake 30 minutes longer.

Remove from oven, sprinkle with walnuts. Bake uncovered 30 minutes longer. Serve with rice pilaf.

Yield: 5-6 servings.

Chicken Scarpariello
"just a little different"

3 whole chicken breasts	2 tablespoons minced chives
2 tablespoons olive oil	¾ cup sliced fresh mushrooms
2 tablespoons butter	1½ cups dry white wine
2 teaspoons salt	½ cup chicken broth
½ teaspoon pepper	½ pound chicken livers
1 clove garlic, minced	2 tablespoons minced parsley

Remove skin and bone chicken; cut into ½-inch pieces.

In large skillet or wok, sauté chicken in 1 tablespoon oil and 1 tablespoon butter. Sprinkle with salt and pepper. Add garlic, chives, mushrooms, wine and chicken broth. Bring to a boil, reduce heat and simmer uncovered over low heat for 30 minutes.

Sauté chicken livers in 1 tablespoon oil and 1 tablespoon butter. Add to chicken mixture; simmer 5 minutes.

Serve over hot wild rice. Sprinkle with parsley.

Yield: 6 servings.

Chicken Supremes
"The sauce makes this easy, elegant dish."

¼ cup butter	½ cup dry white wine, vermouth or champagne
4 boned chicken breast halves, skin removed	1 cup whipping cream
8 oz. fresh mushrooms, sliced	¼ teaspoon salt
4 shallots, sliced, or sliced whites of 4 green onions	⅛ teaspoon white pepper
¼ cup chicken bouillon	Squeeze of lemon juice
	Paprika

Melt butter in skillet; sauté chicken breasts 6-8 minutes, turning. Breasts should still be slightly pink. Remove chicken to hot platter; set aside to keep warm. Place in 200 degree oven during final steps.

In same skillet, reduce fat to 2 tablespoons. Sauté mushrooms and shallots for 2 minutes. Add bouillon and wine. Reduce to a slightly thickened state. Add cream. Bring to boiling point. Add salt and pepper and squeeze of lemon juice.

Serve chicken with sauce; sprinkle with paprika.

Wild rice and kiwi slices make a nice accompaniment.

Yield: 4 servings.

Chicken Breasts with Mustard Persillade

"Persillade is the French word for parsley, the ingredient which offsets the flavor of garlic."

2 cloves garlic
¼ cup butter or margarine
1 cup bread crumbs
1 cup chopped fresh parsley

4 chicken breast halves, skinned and boned
Dijon mustard

Mince garlic; cook in butter in skillet over low heat until soft but not brown. Add bread crumbs and stir until lightly browned. Add parsley; stir and set aside.

Rinse chicken breasts and pat dry with towel. Paint skin side of each breast generously with mustard, as much as you would put on a lightly frosted cake. Dip mustard side of chicken into persillade and press firmly to make crumbs adhere.

Line 13x9x2-inch pan with aluminum foil. Place chicken in pan with space between each piece.

Bake uncovered at 425 degrees for 20-25 minutes until juices run clear when pierced and topping is a deep golden brown. Serve immediately.

Nice served with steamed broccoli, French bread, rice and a lettuce and red onion salad.

Yield: 4 servings.

Northern Italian Baked Chicken

"made in the oven yet similar to batter-fried chicken"

¼ cup vegetable oil
2 tablespoons lemon juice
¼ cup minced green onions
2 tablespoons minced parsley
¾ teaspoon salt
¾ cup flour

½ cup water
¼ cup vegetable oil
¾ teaspoon salt
1 egg white
⅛ teaspoon cream of tartar
3-pound frying chicken, cut up

Mix ¼ cup oil, lemon juice, scallions, parsley and ¾ teaspoon salt. Rub into chicken and let stand at least 2 hours.

One hour before baking, beat together flour, water, ¼ cup oil and ¾ teaspoon salt. Beat egg white until frothy; add cream of tartar; beat until stiff. Fold into flour batter. Dip chicken into batter. Place in greased 13x9x2-inch baking pan.

Bake, uncovered, at 425 degrees for 45 minutes.

Yield: 4 servings.

Diet "Fried" Chicken
"easy, low-calorie recipe"

2½-3 pound frying chicken, cut up   Seasoned salt
¼ cup low-calorie Italian-style
  salad dressing

Remove skin from chicken. Place chicken pieces on rack in baking pan. Brush each piece with dressing. Sprinkle with seasoned salt. Bake at 325 degrees for about 1¼ hours.

Yield: 4 servings.

Honey Mustard Chicken
"good taste and low in cholesterol"

2 teaspoons garlic powder
¼ cup Dijon mustard
Juice of 1 lime

⅓ cup honey
4-5 pounds cut-up frying chicken, skin removed

Stir garlic powder, mustard, lime juice and honey together. Marinate chicken pieces in this mixture at least 1 hour, turning several times.

Bake at 350 degrees for 45 minutes, turning twice. Chicken may also be barbecued or broiled.

Yield: 6-8 servings.

Chicken Imperial
"a good flavor blend"

½ cup margarine
1 teaspoon Worcestershire sauce
½ teaspoon curry powder
½ teaspoon oregano
¼ teaspoon dry mustard
¼ teaspoon garlic powder

⅛ teaspoon paprika
2 dashes Tabasco sauce
¼ cup dry sherry
3-4 pound chicken, cut up and skin removed

Melt margarine with Worcestershire sauce, spices and sherry. Pour over chicken in 13x9x2-inch pan. Bake at 350 degrees for 1 hour, covered; remove cover and bake 30 minutes longer.

Yield: 4-5 servings.

Caribbean Chicken
"a chicken on every grill"

½ cup freshly squeezed lime juice
½ cup soy sauce
½ teaspoon rosemary
½ teaspoon ginger

2 small frying chickens,
   halved or cut up
Melted butter
Lime slices

Mix lime juice, soy sauce, rosemary and ginger. With sharp knife, slash meaty side of chicken pieces to the bone at 1-inch intervals. Place chicken in small casserole; pour marinade over chicken. Marinate 2 hours or overnight in refrigerator, turning occasionally.

Arrange chicken on grill. Brush with butter. Grill pieces 15-20 minutes; brush with marinade several times. Turn, brushing with butter and marinade; cook 15-20 minutes longer. Garnish with lime slices.

Yield: 4-6 servings.

Left Wing of Chicken
"a radical dish"

⅔ cup vegetable oil
4 stalks celery, cut into thin strips
6 sprigs fresh parsley
1 tablespoon tarragon
1 chicken or capon, cut into
   quarters, or 8 leg and
   thigh pieces
Salt

Freshly ground pepper
Nutmeg
20 garlic cloves
⅓ cup cognac
½ teaspoon salt
Water
¾ cup flour
Toast

Pour oil into large casserole. Add celery, parsley and tarragon.

Sprinkle salt, pepper and nutmeg over chicken pieces. Add chicken to vegetable mixture, turning to coat pieces thoroughly. Add garlic, cognac and ½ teaspoon salt. Cover casserole with lid.

Add enough water to flour to make a stiff paste. Make a hermetic seal by spreading flour and water paste on edges of lid and casserole. Completely cover top with aluminum foil.

Bake at 375 degrees for 1½ hours. Do not remove top until ready to serve at the table. Serve with toast to dip in garlic sauce.

Sautéed cabbage makes a delicious accompaniment.

Yield: 4 servings.

Lemon Chicken à la Grecque

"low calorie and elegant"

3-pound chicken, cut up
   (skin removed, optional)
1 tablespoon vegetable oil
3 cloves garlic, minced
1 tablespoon dried chicken
   stock base
1 cup water

¾ pound fresh green beans or
   1 (10 oz.) package frozen
   green beans
2 yellow summer squash, sliced*
3 eggs
3 tablespoons lemon juice

In large skillet, brown chicken in oil. Add garlic, chicken stock base and water. Cover tightly and simmer 25 minutes. Add vegetables and continue cooking 10 minutes more or until tender. Transfer to serving dish and keep warm in oven. Reserve cooking juices.

For sauce, beat eggs until light and airy, about 2-3 minutes. Blend in lemon juice. Gradually add chicken juices, beating constantly with wire whisk. Return to skillet on low heat. Cook and stir until thickened; sauce may curdle if cooked too rapidly. Serve in bowl, or spoon directly over chicken. Serve with rice.

*If summer squash is out of season, substitute 1 additional (10 oz.) package of beans.

Yield: 4-6 servings.

Apple Curry Sauce

"a 'capitol' idea for using up leftover chicken, turkey, or lamb"

¾ cup chopped onion
1½ cups peeled and cubed green
   cooking apples
3 tablespoons butter
2 tablespoons flour
2 teaspoons curry powder
½ teaspoon salt

⅛ teaspoon garlic powder
Few grains nutmeg
Few grains cayenne pepper
1½ cups milk
2 cups cubed cooked meat

Cook onion and apple in butter until transparent, stirring occasionally. Remove from heat. Mix flour and spices together; stir into apple-onion mixture. Gradually add milk. Stirring constantly, bring sauce to a boil. Cook 1 minute. Add meat and cook until heated through.

Serve over hot cooked rice.

Offer a variety of condiments to accompany this dish such as raisins, peanuts, sweet relish, coconut, chopped tomatoes, chopped parsley and chutney.

Yield: 4 servings.

Variation: Sauce without meat may be spooned over sliced, cooked meat. Recipe used this way will serve 8.

Curried Spaghetti with Chicken
"help prevent budget shortfall"

2 (10¾ oz.) cans condensed cream
   of chicken soup
1 (10¾ oz.) can condensed cream
   of mushroom soup
½ cup milk
¼ cup water
½ pound thin spaghetti
2 cups cubed cooked chicken

1 (4½ oz.) can mushrooms,
   drained
2 teaspoons curry powder
¼ teaspoon thyme
⅛ teaspoon oregano
1 (10 oz.) package frozen peas
   and onions, thawed
¼ cup grated Parmesan cheese

In 3-quart saucepan combine soups, milk and ¼ cup water; stir until smooth and simmer while cooking spaghetti. Cook spaghetti in 3 quarts boiling salted water until barely tender.

Add chicken, mushrooms and all seasonings to soup mixture. Simmer 10 minutes. Place spaghetti in 3-quart casserole. Add soup-chicken mixture. Add peas and onions and toss. Sprinkle with Parmesan cheese.

Bake uncovered at 300 degrees for 30 minutes.

Can be made a day ahead, refrigerated and baked for 1 hour.

Yield: 6 servings.

Chicken Livers
"The best you ever ate."

¾ pound chicken livers
¼ cup flour
½ teaspoon salt
¼ teaspoon pepper

¼ cup margarine
⅔ cup mayonnaise
2 tablespoons Worcestershire
   sauce

Coat livers generously with flour which has been seasoned with salt and pepper. In skillet, sauté gently in margarine for not more than 3 minutes on each side and place on a warm serving dish.

Mix mayonnaise and Worcestershire sauce in same skillet and scrape up all the bits of meat. Spoon mixture over livers and toss gently until coated.

Heat oven to 200 degrees; put dish in oven and turn off. Keep in oven at least 15 minutes or up to 45 minutes.

Yield: 2-3 servings, more if served as an appetizer.

Chicken with Pineapple Sauce

"for the Inaugural Ball Banquet"

6 chicken breast halves
Flour
Salt
Pepper
Margarine
1 (20 oz.) can pineapple chunks
1 tablespoon vegetable oil

1 tablespoon soy sauce
½ cup packed brown sugar
¼ cup catsup
3 tablespoons vinegar
1 tablespoon cornstarch
¼ cup water

Coat chicken breasts with flour and put in 13x9x2-inch baking pan. Sprinkle with salt and pepper. Place a small pat of margarine on top of each breast. Bake at 350 degrees for 1 hour.

To prepare sauce, drain pineapple; reserve juice. Combine reserved juice, oil, soy sauce, brown sugar, catsup and vinegar in saucepan. Mix cornstarch and water together and stir into soy sauce mixture. Bring to a boil; cook 1-2 minutes. Stir in pineapple chunks. Pour over chicken. Bake at 325 degrees for 30 minutes longer.

Chopped maraschino cherries and chopped green pepper may be added to sauce for added color and "crunch".

Yield: 6 servings.

Cheddar Turkey Casserole

"recycled"

1 cup quick-cooking white or
   brown rice
2 tablespoons instant minced
   onion
½ (10 oz.) package frozen green
   peas (about 1 cup)
4-6 slices cooked turkey or 2 cups
   diced cooked turkey

1 (10¾ oz.) can condensed
   cheese soup
1 cup milk
1 cup finely crushed cheese
   crackers
3 tablespoons margarine, melted

Prepare rice according to package directions, adding instant minced onion to boiling water. Spread cooked rice in greased 10x6x1½-inch baking dish. Sprinkle with peas, then cover with turkey. Blend soup and milk; pour over turkey. Combine crumbs and margarine; sprinkle over casserole.

Bake at 350 degrees for 35 minutes or until heated through.

Yield: 4-6 servings.

Pheasant and Wild Rice Pilaf

"for peasant pheasant, substitute chicken"

1 garlic clove, minced
1 large onion, diced
1 cup sherry
1 small bay leaf
¼ teaspoon thyme
1 (4 oz.) can mushrooms, drained

1 (4¼ oz.) can chopped ripe
  olives
½ cup consommé, undiluted
1 pheasant, cut up
Flour
2 tablespoons butter or margarine
Wild Rice (below)

Combine garlic, onion, sherry, bay leaf, thyme, mushrooms, ripe olives and consommé. Simmer, covered, for 5 minutes.

Flour pheasant; sauté pieces in butter or margarine in heavy skillet. Remove pheasant to 13x9x2-inch baking pan. Pour soup mixture over pheasant. Bake uncovered at 325 degrees for 1½ hours. Serve with Wild Rice Pilaf.

Yield: 4 servings.

Wild Rice Pilaf

½ cup wild rice
½ cup chopped celery
½ cup chopped onion
1 tablespoon butter or margarine

2 cups chicken broth
1 (4 oz.) can mushrooms
½ cup sliced water chestnuts

Wash wild rice; drain. Put in steamer basket, pour boiling water over rice and cover. Steam rice for about 30 minutes.

Meanwhile, sauté celery and onion in butter. Combine with broth, mushrooms, water chestnuts and rice in casserole; cover. Bake at 350 degrees for about 1½ hours; stir occasionally.

Yield: 4 servings.

Lake-of-the-Woods Fish
"herb-butter baked"

½ cup butter
⅔ cups crushed saltine crackers
¼ cup grated Parmesan cheese
½ teaspoon basil leaves

½ teaspoon oregano
½ teaspoon salt
¼ teaspoon garlic powder
1 pound fish fillets

Melt butter in 13x9x2-inch baking dish. Combine crumbs, cheese and seasonings in flat dish or pie pan. Dip fish fillets in melted butter, then in crumb mixture.

Place fish in the baking dish. Bake at 350 degrees for 25-30 minutes.

Yield: 4 servings.

Baked Fish with Horseradish
"fish with a bite"

½ cup chicken broth
1 tablespoon lemon juice
Salt (optional)
1½ pounds fish fillets
3 tablespoons margarine

2 tablespoons flour
⅓ cup milk or light cream
1 tablespoon prepared horseradish
Chopped parsley

In shallow baking dish, pour broth, juice and salt over fish. Cover and bake at 400 degrees for 10-20 minutes or until fish flakes when tested with a fork.

Let fish cool slightly. Drain juices into measuring cup and add broth, if necessary, to make 1 cup.

Melt margarine in a saucepan; stir in flour and add fish liquid, milk and horseradish to make cream sauce. Bring to a boil, stirring 1-2 minutes or until thick. Spoon sauce over fish.

Bake uncovered at 400 degrees for 10-12 minutes, until sauce is bubbly. Garnish with chopped parsley.

Yield: 3-5 servings.

Paella à la Valenciana

"A one-pot Mediterranean feast."

3 large whole chicken breasts, split, skinned and boned
¼ cup olive oil
½ cup chopped onion
2 cloves garlic, minced
4 large tomatoes, peeled, seeded and cut into eighths
2 sweet red peppers, seeded and cut into eighths
1 teaspoon salt
¼ teaspoon freshly ground pepper

½ teaspoon paprika
2 dozen clams or mussels (can use frozen steamer clams)
¼ cup olive oil
2 cups uncooked rice
1½ pounds shelled and deveined shrimp, fresh or frozen
1 teaspoon saffron
1 (14 oz.) can artichoke hearts, drained and quartered
Chopped fresh parsley

Cut chicken into pieces about 2x1-inch. Heat olive oil in skillet. Sauté chicken about 8 minutes, until no longer pink.

Add onion and garlic, stirring and cooking until tender. Add tomatoes, peppers, salt, pepper and paprika; simmer 5 minutes.

Scrub clams with brush under cold running water. Cover with water in saucepan and simmer until open, about 10 minutes. Remove clams; debeard* while clams remain in shells; set aside. Strain broth through filter paper. Reserve liquid.

Heat remaining oil in another skillet. Sauté rice about 10 minutes until browned. Add chicken and vegetable mixture, shrimp, saffron, artichoke hearts and clam broth (adding enough water to make 4 cups of liquid). Simmer 20 minutes, stirring occasionally, until liquid has been absorbed and rice is tender.

Remove from heat and let stand covered for 10 minutes. Spoon into serving dish or platter. Garnish with clams or mussels in shells; sprinkle with parsley.

*To debeard, work over a bowl to catch juices. Slit skin of the siphon or neck and pull off neck skin, leaving clam in shell. Skin is too tough to eat.

Yield: 8 servings.

Filibuster Fillet

"You'll be talking about this for a long time."

1 pound fish fillets	3 tablespoons margarine
3 tablespoons dry white wine	3 tablespoons flour
2 tablespoons lemon juice	1 cup milk
Salt and pepper to taste	3 tablespoons buttered bread
¼ pound fresh mushrooms, sliced	crumbs
2 tablespoons margarine	2 tablespoons grated Parmesan cheese

Spread fish in buttered casserole and sprinkle with wine, lemon juice, salt and pepper. Cover and bake at 375 degrees for 15 minutes or until fish flakes easily when tested with a fork.

Sauté mushrooms in 2 tablespoons margarine; set aside.

To make cream sauce, melt 3 tablespoons margarine in saucepan over low heat. Blend in flour and milk. Bring to a boil, stirring until mixture is thick. Add mushrooms and liquid from cooked fish.

Pour sauce over fish. Top with crumbs and cheese. Bake another 10 minutes or until bubbly.

Yield: 3-4 servings.

Fish Fritters

"an Icelandic specialty"

1½-2 pounds haddock, flounder or cod fillets	1 teaspoon salt
	Vegetable oil for deep frying

Fritter batter:	
2 cups all-purpose flour	¼ teaspoon pepper
1 teaspoon curry powder	½ teaspoon paprika
½ teaspoon celery salt	2 teaspoons salt
¼ teaspoon garlic salt	¼ cup Pilsner (ale)
¼ teaspoon onion salt	1¼ cups milk

Rinse and drain fillets. Cut into serving size pieces if fillets are large. Sprinkle with salt.

Mix batter ingredients until smooth. Dip fillets into batter for 2-3 minutes.

Heat oil to 350 degrees. Drop fillets, a few at a time, into hot oil and fry until golden brown. Remove and drain on paper towels. Serve with tartar sauce.

Yield: 5-6 servings.

Dilly Turbot
"uff da!"

2 pounds turbot, thawed and cut
   into 6 portions
2 cups boiling water
2 tablespoons lemon juice

1 clove garlic, minced
1 teaspoon salt
Blender Hollandaise Dill Sauce
   (below)

Put fish in greased skillet. Add water, lemon juice, garlic and salt; cover. Simmer until fish flakes easily when tested with a fork, 5-10 minutes.

Carefully remove fish to platter and pour some hot Hollandaise Dill Sauce over fish. Pass remaining sauce.

Yield: 6 servings.

Blender Hollandaise Dill Sauce:

3 egg yolks
2 tablespoons lemon juice

½ tsp. dried dill weed
½ cup butter

Place egg yolks, lemon juice and dill weed in blender. Cover; quickly turn blender on and off.

Heat butter until melted and almost boiling. Turn blender on high speed. Slowly pour in butter, blending until thick and fluffy, about 30 seconds. Hold over warm, not hot, water until ready to serve.

Yield: about ¾ cup.

Whole Wheat Salmon Quiche

"good brunch dish"

1 cup whole wheat flour
⅔ cup shredded sharp
   Cheddar cheese
¼ cup chopped almonds
¼ teaspoon paprika
⅓ cup corn oil
1 (15½ oz.) can salmon
3 eggs, beaten

¼ cup mayonnaise
1 cup dairy sour cream
1 teaspoon lemon juice
½ cup shredded sharp
   Cheddar cheese
¼ teaspoon dill weed
3-5 drops Tabasco sauce

Heat oven to 400 degrees. Combine flour, ⅔ cup cheese, almonds and paprika in quiche or pie pan. Stir in oil. Press mixture onto bottom and side of pan. Bake crust for 10 minutes. Remove from oven and reduce temperature to 325 degrees.

While crust is baking, drain salmon, reserving liquid. Flake salmon; set aside. In bowl, blend eggs, mayonnaise, sour cream, lemon juice and salmon liquid. Stir in salmon, ½ cup cheese, dill weed and Tabasco sauce. Spoon filling into crust.

Bake for 45 minutes or until firm in center. Let stand 5-10 minutes before serving.

Yield: 6-8 servings.

Voyageur Salmon

"a French-Canadian treat"

3 pounds salmon steaks,
   1 inch thick
4 oz. fresh mushrooms, minced
1 medium onion, minced
2 tablespoons fresh parsley,
   minced

¼ cup butter or margarine
½ cup dry sherry
⅓ cup fine bread or corn flake
   crumbs

Place steaks in well-greased shallow casserole.

Mix mushrooms, onion and parsley; spread over fish. Dot with butter. Pour in sherry. Bake at 350 degrees for 15 minutes.

Spread steaks with crumbs and continue baking another 10-15 minutes until fish flakes readily when tested with a fork. Baste 2-3 times during baking.

Serve with parsley-butter potatoes and green beans.

Yield: 6 servings.

Fresh Salmon Vinaigrette
"prepare the night before and serve cold"

1 medium onion, chopped
¼ teaspoon salt
¼ teaspoon sugar
Pepper

1 bay leaf
2 cups vinegar
4 cups water
1 pound salmon steaks,
   1 inch thick

The night before serving, put all ingredients except salmon into kettle and cook rapidly for 25 minutes.

Pour some of the boiling liquid into bottom of casserole that is large enough for the salmon steaks to be placed flat. Lay the salmon steaks gently in liquid and pour remaining liquid over salmon. Bake uncovered at 325 degrees for 25 minutes.

Remove from oven and cool. Cover and refrigerate.

Before serving, carefully remove steaks from liquid, using a spatula. Serve with parsley mayonnaise.

Yield: 2-3 servings.

Seafood Quiche
"for an elegant brunch"

2 (10 oz.) packages frozen
   broccoli, thawed and drained
3 (16 oz.) packages frozen
   crabmeat or shrimp, thawed
   and drained
½ cup sliced green onions
2 (2 oz.) jars pimiento, chopped
1 cup dairy sour cream

1 (8 oz.) package cream cheese,
   softened
1 cup buttermilk baking mix
4 eggs
1 teaspoon Morton's Nature's
   Seasons
Dash of nutmeg
Tomato, thinly sliced
Grated Parmesan cheese

Grease 13x9x2-inch pan or dish. Spread broccoli, crabmeat, onions, and pimiento in pan.

Beat together sour cream, cream cheese, baking mix, eggs and seasonings; pour over mixture in pan. Top with tomato and Parmesan cheese. Bake at 350 degrees for 35 to 40 minutes. Cool 5 minutes before serving.

Yield: 12 servings.

Shrimp Ramequins

"easy and fast"

½ cup butter or margarine
½ pound fresh or frozen cleaned
   shrimp
1 clove garlic, mashed
1 cup sliced fresh mushrooms
1 cup dairy sour cream

2 teaspoons paprika
½ teaspoon salt
1 teaspoon Worcestershire sauce
4 slices Cheddar cheese
Fresh mushrooms
Paprika

Melt butter in skillet; sauté shrimp, garlic and mushrooms until hot.

Mix sour cream with 2 teaspoons paprika, salt and Worcestershire sauce; set aside.

Spoon hot shrimp into ramequin dishes or large scallop shells. Spoon sour cream mixture over top. Cover with cheese. Garnish with fresh mushrooms and sprinkle with paprika.

Bake at 400 degrees until cheese melts.

Yield: 4 servings.

Linguini with Clam Sauce

"a gourmet dish in 20 minutes"

8 oz. linguini
2 (6½ oz.) cans minced clams
¼ cup olive oil
3 cloves garlic, minced
1 tablespoon basil leaves,
   crumbled

Juice of 1 lemon
¼ cup butter
1 tablespoon white wine
1 tablespoon flour

In boiling water, cook linguini *al dente*, according to package directions.

Drain clams; reserve juice.

Heat oil in skillet; cook garlic until light brown. Add clams and basil. Stir in butter and wine; cook gently a few minutes. Add clam juice. Cook and stir. Stir in flour; cook and stir until thickened (no more than 4 minutes).

Yield: 2-3 servings.

OTHER ENTREES

Bureaucratic Beans
"dinner in 20 minutes"

6 slices bacon
1 onion, chopped
1 small green pepper, chopped
4 medium tomatoes, diced
2 (15 oz.) cans kidney beans

1½ tablespoons chili powder
½ teaspoon salt
⅛ teaspoon pepper
2 drops Tabasco sauce
2 cups (8 oz.) shredded
  Cheddar cheese

In large skillet, fry bacon; drain, crumble and set aside.

Using 2 tablespoons bacon fat, sauté onion, green pepper and tomatoes until onions are tender. Add rest of ingredients except bacon; cook over low heat, stirring constantly until cheese melts and mixture is heated through. Sprinkle crumbled bacon over top.

This could be vegetarian if bacon is omitted and oil substituted for bacon fat.

Yield: 4-5 main dish servings; 6-8 side dish servings.

Ratatouille with Eggs
"a terrific eggplant dish"

1 (1 pound) eggplant
1-2 (about 1 pound) zucchini
⅓ cup olive oil
1 cup cubed green pepper
1 cup cubed onion
1 tablespoon minced garlic
2 cups cubed ripe tomatoes

3 tablespoons tomato paste
1 bay leaf
½ teaspoon dried thyme
Salt and pepper to taste
8 eggs
¼ cup freshly grated
  Parmesan cheese

Peel eggplant; cut into 1-inch cubes (about 4 cups). Trim ends of zucchini, but do not peel. Cut into 1-inch cubes (about 4 cups).

Heat oil in heavy range-top casserole. Add eggplant and zucchini; stir-fry for 2 minutes. Add green pepper and onion; stir-fry about 6 minutes. Add garlic and stir. Add tomatoes, tomato paste, bay leaf, thyme, salt and pepper. Bring to a boil, stirring. Bake at 400 degrees for 20 minutes.

Pour mixture into 13x9x2-inch baking dish. Make 8 indentations in ratatouille; break 1 egg into each. Sprinkle cheese evenly over top. Bake 10 minutes longer. Serve immediately.

Yield: 8 servings.

Broiled Sandwiches

"for the time-conscious cook"

1 (2½ oz.) package dried beef, chopped
½ (3 oz.) can chopped ripe olives
1 cup (4 oz.) grated Cheddar cheese

2 drops Tabasco sauce
½ cup mayonnaise
6 English muffin halves or slices of rye bread, toasted

Mix together dried beef, ripe olives, cheese, Tabasco and mayonnaise. Divide mixture evenly among the English muffin halves. Broil until cheese melts. Serve for lunch or after-game snack.

Yield: 3 servings.

Oriental Sandwich

"A cheesy open-faced, vegetarian sandwich."

1 pound fresh bean sprouts, rinsed
1 tablespoon soy sauce
1 cup shredded carrot
¼ cup chopped green onion
¼ cup chopped green pepper

½ teaspoon garlic powder
4 slices whole grain bread, toasted
2 tablespoons butter or margarine
8 slices Cheddar cheese
4 green pepper rings

Toss sprouts with soy sauce; let stand for a few minutes. Drain; stir in vegetables and garlic powder.

Butter toast, top with cheese slice, sprout mixture, another cheese slice. Broil about 4 minutes, until cheese melts. Top with pepper ring.

Yield: 2-4 servings.

Crunchy Vegetable Sandwich

"nutritious and satisfying"

2 leaves Boston lettuce
4 thin slices zucchini
1 thin slice Italian red onion, separated into rings

2 thin slices tomato
2-3 slices Monterey Jack cheese
2 thin slices whole grain bread
2 teaspoons butter or margarine

Layer lettuce, zucchini, onion, tomato and cheese on 1 slice of bread. Top with remaining slice. Melt butter on griddle or skillet over moderate heat.

Sauté sandwich until golden brown, about 5 minutes, turning once and brushing pan with more butter as necessary.

Iceberg lettuce may be used, although it will become more limp.

Yield: 1 serving.

Cheese and Spinach Lasagne
"a meatless alternative"

9 lasagne noodles
1 (12 oz.) package frozen chopped onion
4-6 cloves garlic, crushed
4 (10 oz.) packages frozen chopped spinach, thawed and squeezed almost dry
2 tablespoons olive oil

Freshly ground pepper to taste
2 pounds dry cottage or ricotta cheese
7 cups (1¾ pounds) shredded or sliced mozzarella cheese
2 cups (8 oz.) freshly grated Parmesan cheese
Ripe olives, chopped

Cook noodles according to package directions; do not overcook.
Sauté onion and garlic with spinach in olive oil until heated through. Add pepper to taste.

Grease 13x9x2-inch pan with olive oil. Put 3 noodles in bottom, then one-third of spinach mixture; crumble on one-third of dry cottage cheese, then one-third of mozzarella cheese and one-third of Parmesan cheese. Repeat layering process two more times, using all ingredients. Garnish with olives. Bake at 350 degrees about 40 minutes.

Yield: 8 servings.

Yankee Doodle Noodles
"a sweet accompaniment for dinner"

1 pound medium noodles, cooked
1 cup dairy sour cream
½ cup sugar
Pinch of salt
4 eggs, beaten

1 cup creamed cottage cheese
1 teaspoon vanilla
¼ teaspoon cinnamon
½ cup raisins

Glaze:
¼ cup butter or margarine
1 cup packed brown sugar

1 cup pecan halves

Rinse cooked noodles with cold water; drain. Add remaining ingredients, except ingredients for glaze, mixing well.

Melt butter for glaze in 13x9x2-inch pan. Sprinkle brown sugar evenly over butter. Press pecans into brown sugar. Pour in noodle mixture.

Bake at 350 degrees for 1 hour or until set. Cool in pan for 10 minutes. Run knife around edges to loosen; invert onto serving plate. Let cool for 10 minutes more before removing pan.

Yield: 12 servings.

Stuffed Pasta

"Bravo! — worth every minute of preparation."

1 pound jumbo pasta shells (plain or whole wheat)	2 teaspoons minced fresh parsley or ½ teaspoon dried parsley
1½ pounds ricotta or cottage cheese	2 eggs
3 cups (12 oz.) shredded mozzarella cheese	Tomato Sauce (below)
1 teaspoon salt	¼ cup (1 oz.) shredded mozzarella cheese

Parcook shells in boiling water; drain dry on towel.

Mix ricotta, 3 cups mozzarella cheese, salt, parsley and eggs. Stuff into each shell.

Pour a thin layer of Tomato Sauce on bottom of 13x9x2-inch casserole or baking pan. Arrange layer of shells; cover with sauce. Repeat layers of shells and sauce, ending with sauce. Sprinkle ¼ cup mozzarella cheese on top.

Cover and bake at 350 degrees for 45 minutes.

Yield: 4-6 servings.

Tomato Sauce:

¾ cup chopped onion	1 teaspoon salt
1 clove garlic, crushed	1 bay leaf
3 tablespoons vegetable oil	2 (16 oz.) cans tomatoes
8 oz. fresh mushrooms, sliced	2 (6 oz.) cans tomato paste
1½ teaspoons oregano	¾ teaspoon sugar
⅛ teaspoon pepper	¾ teaspoon cinnamon

In large skillet, sauté onion and garlic in oil until almost tender. Add mushrooms and sauté until all ingredients are tender but not brown.

Add remaining ingredients; simmer uncovered 30 minutes. Remove bay leaf. Cover and simmer another 30 minutes.

Yield: 2 quarts.

Meatless Manicotti
"Early decision: this is great!"

10 manicotti shells
3 cups diced zucchini
2 tablespoons butter or margarine
1½ cups cottage cheese
1 cup (4 oz.) shredded Cheddar
  cheese

1 (1½ oz.) envelope Sloppy Joe
  seasoning mix
1 (6 oz.) can tomato paste
1½ cups boiling water
½ cup (2 oz.) shredded Cheddar
  cheese

Cook manicotti shells in 4 quarts salted boiling water until almost tender, about 10 minutes. Drain and rinse in cold water.

Cook zucchini in butter in large skillet, about 10 minutes. Add cottage cheese and 1 cup Cheddar cheese.

Stuff manicotti shells with cheese mixture. Arrange in single layer in shallow 2-quart baking pan.

Stir together seasoning mix, tomato paste and water. Spoon over manicotti. Cover with foil and bake at 375 degrees for 30 minutes.

Uncover; sprinkle with remaining ½ cup cheese and bake 10-15 minutes longer, until hot and bubbly.

Can be prepared ahead and frozen ready for baking.

Yield: 4-5 servings.

Brazilian Rice
"good luncheon entrée or dinner side dish"

¼ cup butter, melted
4 eggs, beaten
4 cups (1 pound) shredded
  sharp Cheddar cheese
1 cup milk
1 (10 oz.) package frozen
  chopped spinach, cooked
  and well drained

1 tablespoon chopped onion
1 tablespoon Worcestershire
  sauce
½ teaspoon marjoram
½ teaspoon thyme
½ teaspoon rosemary
3 cups cooked rice

Combine butter, eggs, cheese, milk, spinach, onion and spices; stir into rice. Pour into 2-quart baking dish. Place dish in pan of hot water. Bake at 350 degrees for 45 minutes .

Yield: 8 servings.

Mixed Rice with Vegetables
"high-protein vegetarian main dish"

½ cup wild rice
½ cup brown rice
1 teaspoon basil
¼ teaspoon garlic powder
1 tablespoon instant
  vegetable bouillon
3 cups water
3 tablespoons vegetable oil
2 cups sliced celery
1 cup broccoli stems and
  flowerets
1 cup sliced carrots
1 cup cauliflowerets

8 large fresh mushrooms, sliced
4 oz. Chinese pea pods
2 medium onions, quartered
1 (8 oz.) can sliced water
  chestnuts, drained
1 cup slivered almonds
¼ teaspoon garlic powder
2 tablespoons soy sauce
¾ cup plain yogurt
1 cup (4 oz.) shredded
  Monterey Jack cheese
1 cup (4 oz.) shredded
  Cheddar cheese

Wash wild rice; drain. Combine rices, basil, ¼ teaspoon garlic powder, instant vegetable bouillon and water. Cook over low heat until rice is tender, 30-40 minutes.

Heat oil in wok or large skillet. Add ingredients to wok at 2 minutes intervals, as follows: celery; broccoli, carrots and cauliflower; mushrooms, pea pods and onions; water chestnuts; almonds. Add ¼ teaspoon garlic powder, soy sauce and yogurt. Toss lightly.

Spread rice in greased 2½-quart casserole. Cover with vegetable mixture; sprinkle with cheese. Bake at 400 degrees for 20 minutes.

Yield: 6 servings.

Tofu with Rice
"Try this if you have never eaten tofu before."

½ cup chopped onion
½ cup chopped celery
½ cup sliced fresh mushrooms
½ cup chopped carrots
2 tablespoons vegetable oil
½ cup coarsely chopped cashews

1 (1 pound) package tofu,
  drained and crumbled
½ cup soy sauce
1½ cups cooked rice
1 cup (4 oz.) shredded Cheddar
  cheese (optional)

Sauté onion, celery, mushrooms and carrots in oil. Combine with other ingredients except cheese. Place in greased 13x9x2-inch baking dish. Sprinkle with cheese. Bake at 350 degrees for 20-30 minutes.

Yield: 6 servings.

Monterey Zucchini Casserole

"attractive dish with a mild, cheesy taste"

3 cups cooked rice
1 (7 oz.) or 2 (4 oz.) cans chopped
 green chilies, drained
8 oz. sliced Monterey Jack cheese
3 medium zucchini, sliced
 ¼ inch thick
3 large tomatoes, peeled and
 sliced

2 cups dairy sour cream
1 teaspoon oregano
1 teaspoon garlic salt
¼ cup chopped green pepper
¼ cup chopped green onion
1 tablespoon minced parsley
8 oz. shredded Monterey Jack
 cheese

Place rice in greased 13x9x2-inch baking dish. Add layer of chilies. Layer sliced cheese over chilies. Place zucchini slices over cheese and top with tomato slices.

Mix sour cream with oregano, garlic salt, green pepper, onion and parsley. Spoon over tomatoes, spreading out as much as possible. Sprinkle shredded cheese on sour cream mixture. Bake at 350 degrees about 30 minutes or until hot and bubbly.

Yield: 6-8 servings.

Rice with Green Chilies

"unusual main dish with chilies and cheese"

1 cup rice
2 cups water
1½ teaspoons instant
 chicken bouillon
1 cup dairy sour cream
1 (4 oz.) can diced green chilies,
 drained

¼ cup (1 oz.) shredded Monterey
 Jack or Muenster cheese
Salt and pepper to taste
½ teaspoon marjoram
½ cup grated Parmesan cheese
Fresh tomato wedges

In covered saucepan, cook rice in water with bouillon for 20 minutes or until rice is tender and all bouillon is absorbed.

Mix rice, sour cream, green chilies, cheese, salt, pepper and marjoram. Place on oval baking platter or shallow 1½-quart casserole. Sprinkle with Parmesan cheese.

Arrange tomato wedges around edge of platter. Press into rice to form secure border. Bake, covered with foil, at 350 degrees for 25-30 minutes.

Yield: 4 servings.

Herbs, Chicken and Rice Casserole

"Herbs are a natural complement to wild rice."

1 small onion, chopped	¼ teaspoon basil
1 clove garlic, crushed	1 tablespoon parsley flakes
2 tablespoons oil	¼ teaspoon sage
½ cup wild rice	⅛ teaspoon pepper
1 stalk celery, chopped	½ cup long-grain rice
½ cup chopped green pepper	½ cup sliced water chestnuts
½ cup thinly sliced fresh	½ cup slivered almonds
mushrooms (optional)	3 tablespoons chopped pimiento
3 cups chicken or turkey broth	½-1 cup dairy sour cream
1-2 cups cooked, chopped	
chicken or turkey	

Wash wild rice; drain. Sauté onion and garlic in oil until transparent; add wild rice. When rice is coated with oil, add celery, green pepper, mushrooms, broth, chicken, basil, parsley, sage and pepper. Bake in covered 2½-quart casserole at 350 degrees for 45 minutes.

Remove from oven; stir in long grain rice, water chestnuts, almonds, pimiento and sour cream. Bake 45 minutes longer.

Yield: 6 servings.

Variation: Cut-up beef and beef broth may be substituted for chicken and chicken broth; omit sage.

Oriental Wild Rice Casserole

"makes the simplest meal special"

½ cup wild rice	¼ cup soy sauce
2½ cups boiling water	4 oz. fresh mushrooms, sliced
½ cup long-grain rice	1 (8 oz.) can sliced water
1 cup chopped celery	chestnuts, drained
1 cup chopped onion	⅓ cup slivered toasted almonds
3 tablespoons butter or margarine	

Wash wild rice; drain. Add to boiling water. Cover and simmer 20 minutes. Add long grain rice; cover and simmer 20 minutes more.

Sauté vegetables in butter until tender. Combine all ingredients. Bake in 1½-quart casserole at 350 degrees for 20 minutes or at 300 degrees for 1 hour.

Yield: 8 servings.

Pullao

*"translates as pilaf and is traditionally made with long grain rice
and sweetly aromatic spices"*

2 cups rice
2 cups boiling water
1 tablespoon margarine
4 whole cloves
1-inch piece of cinnamon stick
½ teaspoon turmeric
2 cups chicken broth

1 tablespoon dried mint
1 tablespoon fresh gingerroot
½ cup slivered almonds or cashews
½ cup golden raisins
½ cup plain yogurt

Soak rice in boiling water for 5 minutes; drain. Heat margarine and sauté cloves, cinnamon stick and turmeric. Add drained rice, chicken broth and remaining ingredients. Cover and simmer about 15-20 minutes.

Yield: 4 servings.

Wild Rice Casserole

"the natural wild rice flavor comes through"

1 cup wild rice
½ cup butter or margarine
3 tablespoons grated onion
½ cup slivered almonds

8 oz. fresh mushrooms, sliced
3 cups chicken or beef broth
(or 3 bouillon cubes dissolved in 3 cups hot water)

Wash rice; drain. Sauté rice, onions and almonds in butter; add mushrooms. Pour into 3-quart casserole; add broth. Cover and bake at 325 degrees for 1½ hours.

Yield: 8-10 servings.

White House Rice

"served at a White House Buffet featuring states' products"

1 cup wild rice
1 cup (4 oz.) shredded cheese (Cheddar and/or Monterey Jack)
1 cup halved ripe olives
1 (16 oz.) can tomatoes

1 (4 oz.) can mushrooms, undrained
½ cup onion flakes
½ cup olive oil
1½ teaspoons salt
½ cup boiling water

Wash rice; drain. Combine all ingredients and place in greased covered 2½-quart casserole. Bake at 375 degrees for 2-2½ hours.

A pound of cooked ground beef may be added to make a main dish.

Yield: 6 servings.

Baked Cheese Fondue
"prepared completely in advance"

11 (½-inch) slices French Bread
Butter, softened
1 medium onion, grated
1 large carrot, shredded
¼ cup minced parsley
Chives to taste
Thyme to taste
Basil to taste

2 cups (8 oz.) shredded sharp
 Cheddar cheese
4 eggs
2½ cups milk
2 tablespoons Dijon mustard
1 teaspoon Worcestershire sauce
⅛ teaspoon paprika
Mushroom Dill Sauce (optional,
 below)

Spread 10 slices of bread with butter. Cut into 1-inch cubes. Place half of cubes in 2-quart soufflé dish and sprinkle with half of onion, carrot, herbs and cheese. Repeat layer.

Butter and cube remaining slice of bread and mound in center of dish. Beat eggs with milk, mustard, Worcestershire sauce and paprika. Pour over bread-cheese mixture.

Cover and refrigerate overnight. Remove from refrigerator and let stand at room temperature 45 minutes.

Bake at 350 degrees for 1 hour or until puffed and golden brown. Serve with Mushroom Dill Sauce if desired.

Yield: 4-6 servings.

Mushroom Dill Sauce:

8 oz. fresh mushrooms, sliced
¼ cup chopped green onion
¼ cup butter
1 tablespoon paprika
 (preferably Hungarian)
¼ cup flour

1 teaspoon seasoned salt
½ teaspoon dill weed
Dash of pepper
Dash of Tabasco sauce
1½ cups half and half cream
2 teaspoons lemon juice

Sauté mushrooms and green onion in butter. Remove from heat; add seasonings. Slowly stir in cream. Bring to a boil; cook and stir 1 minute. Stir in lemon juice.

Yield: about 3 cups.

French Toast Sandwiches with Chilies, Ham and Cheese

"a new twist on an old favorite"

1 (4 oz.) can chopped green
   chilies, drained and rinsed
1 cup finely chopped cooked ham
2 cups (8 oz.) shredded Monterey
   Jack, sharp Cheddar or
   Muenster cheese

8 slices white bread
5 eggs
1¾ cups milk
½ teaspoon chili powder
½ teaspoon dry mustard
Salt to taste

Mix together chilies, ham and 1 cup cheese. Divide mixture into 4 equal portions and spread over 4 bread slices. Cover with remaining bread slices to make 4 sandwiches; place in well-buttered 9x9x2-inch pan (trim crusts if necessary so all will fit).

Beat eggs until blended; beat in milk, chili powder, mustard and salt. Pour mixture over sandwiches. Cover and refrigerate at least 2 hours or overnight.

Uncover sandwiches and sprinkle evenly with remaining cup cheese. Bake at 350 degrees for 35-40 minutes or until puffed and light brown. Serve at once.

Yield: 4 servings.

Spanish Tortilla

"A hearty and quick brunch dish."

2 cups vegetable oil
9 potatoes (2½ pounds)
2 large green peppers,
   cut into 1-inch pieces
1 teaspoon salt

12 oz. chorizos or pepperoni,
   sliced (optional)
8 eggs, beaten
1 (4 oz.) jar chopped pimiento,
   drained

Heat oil in 12-inch teflon skillet over medium heat. Peel, wash, dry and dice potatoes. Fry all potatoes at once until soft, not brown. Add salt and green pepper and cook until peppers are tender.

Add layer of chorizos; do not stir. When chorizos are soft, gently mix together. Drain off all oil. Reduce heat and add eggs. Cook until dry.

Invert a plate over skillet, turn out tortilla; return tortilla to pan to brown other side. When cooked dry, remove from skillet by inverting a plate over skillet. Garnish with pimiento.

Yield: 6-8 servings.

Eggs Sardou
"serve for a special breakfast with friends"

2 cups fresh or cooked spinach   **4 artichoke bottoms**
4 eggs, poached   **Hollandaise Sauce (below)**

For each serving, make a bed of spinach on a salad plate. Place artichoke bottom on spinach and poached egg on artichoke. Cover all with Hollandaise Sauce.

Serve with toasted and buttered English muffins.

Yield: 4 servings.

Hollandaise Sauce:

½ cup butter   **Few grains cayenne pepper**
4 egg yolks, well beaten   **½ teaspoon salt**
¼ cup boiling water   **2 tablespoons lemon juice**

Melt butter in top of double boiler over simmering water. Water should be at least ½ inch from bottom of top of double boiler. Gradually beat in yolks with wire whisk. Very slowly add boiling water while beating continuously. Beat until mixture thickens and coats whisk or metal spoon.

Remove sauce from heat and beat in cayenne pepper, salt and lemon juice.

If sauce overcooks and starts to separate, immediately remove pan from double boiler, set pan in ice water and continue to beat until smooth.

Yield: about 1 cup.

Funny Eggs

"a top-of-the-stove almost-quiche"

½ cup cottage cheese
3 eggs
¼ cup grated Parmesan cheese
¼ teaspoon salt
⅛ teaspoon freshly ground
    pepper

½-1 cup chopped fresh or frozen
    vegetables of your choice
3 tablespoons chopped bacon
1 cup (4 oz.) shredded cheese of
    your choice

Push cottage cheese through sieve into mixing bowl. Add eggs and beat well. Add Parmesan cheese, salt and pepper; mix thoroughly. Add raw vegetable pieces and stir to coat with egg mixture.

Fry bacon in 9-inch skillet over medium heat until very crisp. Drain bacon on paper towels. Pour off all but 1 tablespoon fat. Pour in egg-vegetable mixture and turn heat to low. Top eggs with cheese and sprinkle with crumbled bacon.

Cover and cook until set, about 15 minutes. Cut in wedges to serve.

Yield: 2-3 servings.

CAKES & COOKIES ☑

Almond Butter Cookies
"melt-in-your-mouth"

4 oz. whole blanched almonds
1 cup butter
1 cup sugar
2 egg yolks
½ teaspoon lemon extract

¾ teaspoon vanilla
¾ teaspoon almond extract
2 cups all-purpose flour
1 teaspoon baking powder
⅛ teaspoon salt

Toast almonds at 350 degrees for 15 minutes; set aside.

Heat oven to 300 degrees. Cream butter and sugar together until light and fluffy. Add egg yolks, one at a time, beating well after each addition. Blend in lemon, vanilla and almond extract. Stir flour, baking powder and salt together; add to creamed mixture; mix thoroughly.

Form dough into 1-inch balls. Place balls on an ungreased cookie sheet about 2 inches apart and press an almond in center of each.

Bake for 15-20 minutes until edges just begin to brown. Cool 5 minutes; remove to racks.

Yield: 4½ dozen.

Christmas Balls
"colorful on a tray of cookies"

1 cup margarine or butter,
  softened
2 teaspoons vanilla
⅓ cup granulated sugar

2 teaspoons water
2 cups all-purpose flour
1 cup finely chopped pecans
Red and green decorator sugar

Heat oven to 325 degrees. Cream margarine and vanilla. Add sugar; cream until light and fluffy. Blend in water. Stir in flour, mixing well. Add pecans.

Shape dough into 1-inch balls. Roll each ball in decorator sugar. Place 1 inch apart on ungreased cookie sheet. Bake for 20 minutes or until firm to the touch. Cool before removing from pan.

Yield: 3-4 dozen.

Sour Cream Drops
"for the tea table or the lunchbox"

½ cup butter, softened
1½ cups sugar
2 eggs
1 cup dairy sour cream
1 teaspoon vanilla

2¾ cups all-purpose flour
½ teaspoon baking soda
½ teaspoon salt
½ teaspoon baking powder
Brown Butter Icing (below)

Heat oven to 425 degrees. Cream butter and sugar together until light and fluffy. Beat in eggs. Stir in sour cream and vanilla. Stir dry ingredients together and stir thoroughly into batter.

Drop by teaspoonfuls onto ungreased cookie sheet. Bake for 8-10 minutes. Cool and frost with Browned Butter Icing.

Yield: 5 dozen 2½-inch cookies.

Variation: Brown sugar may be substituted for granulated sugar; ⅔ cup raisins and ½ cup nuts may be stirred in at end.

Browned Butter Icing:

¼ cup butter, softened
2 cups powdered sugar

2 tablespoons half and half cream
1 teaspoon vanilla

Blend sugar and butter together. Add cream and vanilla and beat until smooth.

Yield: about 1 cup.

Peanut Butter Chocolate Stars
"staff loved these"

1 cup peanut butter
1 cup sugar

1 egg
48 chocolate star candies

Heat oven to 350 degrees. Mix peanut butter, sugar and egg together to form dough. Drop dough by teaspoonfuls on ungreased cookie sheet; press chocolate star on top of each cookie. Bake for 12-15 minutes. Cool 4 minutes before removing from cookie sheet.

Yield: 3½-4 dozen.

Consensus Cookies
"best ever"

1 cup margarine, softened
1 cup granulated sugar
1 cup packed brown sugar
1 cup vegetable oil
1 egg
2 teaspoons vanilla
3½ cups all-purpose flour

1 teaspoon baking soda
1 teaspoon cream of tartar
1 teaspoon salt
1 cup Rice Krispies
1 cup rolled oats
1 cup shredded coconut

Heat oven to 350 degrees. Cream margarine and sugars; add oil, egg and vanilla. Beat well.

Stir flour, baking soda, cream of tartar and salt together and add to creamed mixture. Beat thoroughly. Stir in cereals and coconut.

Shape rounded teaspoonfuls of dough into balls; flatten on ungreased cookie sheet. Bake for 10 minutes.

Yield: 6½ dozen.

Blackstrap Molasses Cookies
"a family favorite for 5 generations"

1 cup sugar
1 cup shortening
1 cup blackstrap molasses
2 eggs, beaten
1 tablespoon baking soda
1 cup dairy sour cream

½ teaspoon salt
2 tablespoons baking powder
1 tablespoon cinnamon
1 tablespoon ginger
4 cups all-purpose flour

Heat oven to 375 degrees. Mix ingredients together in order given to form dough.

Drop by teaspoonfuls onto greased cookie sheet. Flatten with bottom of glass that has been greased and dipped in granulated sugar. (Dip glass for each cookie.) Bake for 10-15 minutes.

Yield: 5 dozen.

Praline Cookies
"always chosen first"

½ cup margarine, softened	2 cups all-purpose flour
⅔ cup packed dark brown sugar	½ teaspoon baking soda
1 egg	¼ teaspoon salt
½ teaspoon vanilla	1 cup broken walnuts or pecans
½ teaspoon maple flavoring	Brown Sugar Frosting (below)

Cream margarine and sugar; add egg and flavorings and beat well. Stir flour, salt and baking soda together. Stir into sugar mixture. Chill dough.

Shape dough into roll about 12 inches long; wrap in aluminum foil. Refrigerate at least 4 hours.

Heat oven to 350 degrees. Cut dough in ⅛-¼-inch thick slices; place on greased cookie sheet. Gently press 4-6 nut pieces into each cookie. Bake about 10 minutes. Cool; frost with Brown Sugar Frosting.

Yield: 4 dozen.

Brown Sugar Frosting:

½ cup packed dark brown sugar	1 cup powdered sugar
1 tablespoon light corn syrup	1 tablespoon water
1 tablespoon water	

In a saucepan, heat brown sugar, corn syrup and 1 tablespoon water to boiling, stirring constantly. Add powdered sugar and 1 tablespoon water. Beat until of spreading consistency. If frosting hardens, add a drop or two of water and reheat.

Yield: about 1 cup.

Monster Cookies
"favorite cookie of the Senator's staff"

1 pound butter, softened
3 pounds crunchy peanut butter
2 pounds brown sugar
4 cups granulated sugar
1 dozen eggs
1 tablespoon vanilla

1 tablespoon light corn syrup
3 tablespoons baking soda
18 cups rolled oats
1 (12 oz.) package chocolate chips
1 (16 oz.) package M&M candies

Heat oven to 350 degrees. In very large bowl cream butter, peanut butter and sugars. Add eggs, vanilla and syrup; beat well. Combine rolled oats and baking soda; add to creamed mixture. Stir in chocolate chips and M&M candies.

Drop dough by ⅓ cupfuls onto greased cookie sheet, 6 per cookie sheet. Slightly flatten each mound of dough. Bake for 10 minutes. Recipe may be easily halved.

Yield: 7 dozen 5-inch cookies.

Chocolate Cherry Cake
"GNO — Gross National Obsession"

2 cups sugar
⅔ cup butter
2 eggs, beaten
1 (10 oz.) jar maraschino cherries, quartered
¼ cup maraschino cherry juice

1¾ cups buttermilk
2 (1 oz.) squares unsweetened chocolate, melted
3 cups cake flour
2 teaspoons baking soda
Fudge Frosting (below)

Heat oven to 350 degrees. Cream sugar and butter until light and fluffy. Beat in eggs.

Combine cherry juice and buttermilk. Stir flour and baking soda together. Add alternately with buttermilk to creamed mixture, beating after each addition. Stir in melted chocolate. Fold in cherries.

Pour batter into two greased and floured baking pans, one 13x9x2-inch and one 8x8x2-inch. Bake for 30 minutes. Cool and frost with Fudge Frosting.

Yield: One 13x9-inch cake and one 8x8-inch cake or three 9-inch round layers.

Fudge Frosting:

3 cups sugar
3 tablespoons light corn syrup
¼ teaspoon salt
1 cup milk

2 (1 oz.) squares unsweetened
 chocolate
¼ cup butter
1 teaspoon vanilla

Mix sugar, corn syrup, salt, milk and chocolate together in 2-quart saucepan. Cook and stir over low heat until sugar dissolves. Cook to soft ball stage (232 degrees).

Remove from heat. Add butter and vanilla; do not stir. Allow to cool undisturbed until bottom of pan feels warm to touch. Beat until icing just begins to lose its shiny appearance.

Yield: Enough to frost one 13x9-inch cake and one 8x8-inch cake or one 9-inch 3-layer cake.

Hundred Dollar Chocolate Cake
"good for a fund raiser"

2 cups whole wheat pastry flour
1 cup sugar
¼ cup cocoa
2 teaspoons baking soda

Dash of salt
1 cup water
1 cup salad dressing or
 mayonnaise

Heat oven to 350 degrees. Stir dry ingredients together. Slowly stir in water. Fold in salad dressing. Pour batter into 2 greased and floured 9-inch round layer pans or one 13x9x2-inch cake pan.

Bake for 30-40 minutes. Cool.

This cake recipe can be doubled and baked in the same size pan. Excellent with Peanut Butter Frosting (below).

Yield: One 9-inch 2-layer or one 13x9x2-inch cake.

Peanut Butter Frosting:

3 cups powdered sugar
⅓ cup margarine, softened
⅓ cup peanut butter

1 teaspoon vanilla
2-3 tablespoons milk

Mix powdered sugar, margarine and peanut butter together. Add vanilla. Add milk and beat until light and fluffy.

Yield: Frosts one 2-layer or one 13x9-inch cake.

Banana Ripple Cake

"delicious combination of banana, chocolate and cherry"

½ cup chocolate chips
¼ cup water
½ cup butter
1¼ cups sugar
2 eggs, separated
2 cups all-purpose flour
¾ teaspoon baking soda
½ teaspoon salt

¼ teaspoon baking powder
1 cup mashed ripe banana
⅓ cup dairy sour cream
1 teaspoon vanilla
⅓ cup chopped maraschino cherries, drained
¼ cup sugar

Melt chocolate with water in top of double boiler; set aside to cool. Heat oven to 350 degrees. Cream butter and 1¼ cup sugar until light and fluffy. Add egg yolks; beat thoroughly.

Stir flour, baking soda, salt and baking powder together. Mix banana with sour cream and vanilla. Add to creamed mixture alternately with dry ingredients, beating after each addition. Stir in cherries.

Beat egg whites until very soft peaks form; gradually beat in ¼ cup sugar and continue beating until stiff but not dry. Gently fold beaten egg whites into batter.

Place one-third of batter in greased and floured 10-inch tube pan. Drizzle half of chocolate over batter. Repeat with one-third of batter and remaining chocolate. Top with remaining batter. Bake for 1 hour.

Yield: One 10-inch tube cake.

Celebration Cake

"let the good times roll"

3 cups all-purpose flour
2 cups sugar
1 teaspoon baking soda
1 teaspoon salt
1 teaspoon cinnamon
1⅓ cups vegetable oil

3 eggs, beaten
1½ teaspoons vanilla
1 (8 oz.) can crushed pineapple
2 cups chopped bananas
1 cup chopped pecans or walnuts
Cream Cheese Frosting (below)

Heat oven to 350 degrees. In large bowl, combine dry ingredients. Add oil and eggs, stirring only enough to mix. Stir in vanilla, pineapple and juice, bananas and nuts. Pour into 3 greased and floured 9-inch round layer pans. Bake for 25 minutes. Frost with Cream Cheese Frosting.

Yield: One 9-inch 3-layer cake.

Cream Cheese Frosting:

1 (8 oz.) package cream cheese, softened
½ cup butter or margarine, softened

1 pound powdered sugar
1 teaspoon vanilla
½ cup chopped pecans or walnuts (optional)

Combine all ingredients except nuts. Beat until light and fluffy. Spread between layers and on top of cake. Sprinkle nuts over top of cake.

Yield: Frosts a 9-inch 3-layer cake.

Italian Cream Cake

"stuff the ballot box with votes for this"

½ cup butter, softened
½ cup shortening
1 teaspoon vanilla
2 cups sugar
5 eggs, separated
2 cups all-purpose flour

1 teaspoon baking soda
½ teaspoon salt
1 cup buttermilk
1 cup chopped pecans
1 (3½ oz.) can coconut

Heat oven to 325 degrees. Cream butter, shortening, vanilla and sugar until light and fluffy. Add egg yolks one at a time, beating after each addition.

Stir dry ingredients together. Alternate dry ingredients with buttermilk, beating after each addition.

Beat egg whites until very soft peaks form. Fold into cake mixture. Fold in pecans and coconut. Turn into three 8-inch greased and floured round layer pans. Bake for 25 minutes.

Cool and frost with Cream Cheese Frosting.

Yield: One 8-inch 3-layer cake.

English Delight

"white cake with carmelized nuts topped with whipped cream and a tangy lemon sauce"

1 cup packed brown sugar
1 cup chopped pecans
½ cup butter, melted

1 (18.5 oz.) package white cake mix
1 cup whipping cream, whipped
Lemon Sauce (below)

Heat oven to 325 degrees. Prepare 13x9x2-inch cake pan by greasing, lining with waxed paper and greasing waxed paper. Combine brown sugar, pecans and butter. Pat mixture into bottom of pan.

Prepare cake mix according to package directions; pour over nut mixture. Bake 40-45 minutes.

Remove cake from pan immediately, inverting onto tray or cookie sheet. While still warm, cut cake into 15 (3x5-inch) pieces.

To serve, place cake on dessert plates, top with a spoonful of whipped cream; pour about ⅓ cup warm Lemon Sauce over each serving.

Yield: 15 (3 × 5-inch) servings.

Lemon Sauce:

1½ cups sugar
5 tablespoons cornstarch
3 cups water
½ cup lemon juice

¼ cup butter
1 teaspoon lemon peel
Yellow food coloring (optional)

Combine sugar and cornstarch in a saucepan. Add water and lemon juice, stirring until sugar is dissolved.

Bring to a boil and cook until clear and thickened, 1-2 minutes. Remove from heat; stir in butter and lemon peel. Stir in a few drops of food coloring.

Yield: about 4½ cups.

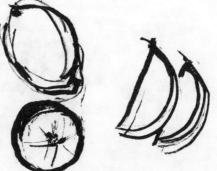

Blueberry Batter Cake
"try with raspberries, too"

2 cups blueberries	⅛ teaspoon salt
Juice of ½ lemon	½ cup milk
¾ cup sugar	1 cup sugar
3 tablespoons margarine	1 tablespoon cornstarch
1 cup all-purpose flour	½ teaspoon salt
1 teaspoon baking powder	1 cup boiling water

Heat oven to 375 degrees. Place blueberries in greased 8x8x2-inch pan. Sprinkle with lemon juice.

Cream ¾ cup sugar and margarine. Stir flour, baking powder and ⅛ teaspoon salt together. Add alternately with milk to creamed mixture, beating after each addition. Pour over berries.

Combine 1 cup sugar, cornstarch and ½ teaspoon salt; sprinkle over top of batter. Pour boiling water over all. Bake for 1 hour.

Serve warm topped with vanilla ice cream or a dollop of whipped cream, if desired.

Yield: 6 servings.

Campaigner's Carrot Cake
"a winner"

1¾ cups sugar	2 teaspoons baking soda
1½ cups vegetable oil	2 teaspoons cinnamon
4 eggs	3 cups shredded carrots
2¼ cups all-purpose flour	1½ cups chopped walnuts
1 teaspoon salt	

Heat oven to 300 degrees. In mixer bowl, combine sugar, oil and eggs; beat at medium speed 2 minutes.

Stir together flour, salt, baking soda and cinnamon. Add to batter; beat 2 minutes more. Add carrots and walnuts to batter; beat 1 minute more.

Pour batter into greased and floured 15x10x1-inch pan. Bake for 1 hour. Cool and frost with Cream Cheese Frosting.

Yield: 36 pieces.

Variation: One cup coconut may be substituted for 1 cup of carrots.

Mandarin Orange Cake
"mandated by all"

2 eggs
2 (11½ oz.) cans mandarin
   oranges, drained
2 cups granulated sugar
2 cups all-purpose flour
2 teaspoons baking soda

2 teaspoons vanilla
½ teaspoon salt
¾ cup packed brown sugar
3 tablespoons milk
3 tablespoons butter

Heat oven to 350 degrees. In large bowl, beat eggs; add oranges, granulated sugar, flour, baking soda, vanilla and salt. Beat on low speed for 4 minutes.

Pour batter into greased and floured 13x9x2-inch baking pan. Bake for 30-35 minutes.

Toward end of baking time, bring brown sugar, milk and butter to boil in small saucepan. Boil 3 minutes.

When cake is done, remove from oven and poke holes in it. Pour hot sugar mixture over cake. Cool.

Serve topped with whipped cream, if desired.

Yield: One 13x9-inch cake.

Brandy Apple Cake with Sauce
"disappears as fast as a campaign promise"

¼ cup shortening
1 cup sugar
1 egg
¼ teaspoon salt
1 teaspoon cinnamon
1 teaspoon nutmeg
1 teaspoon baking soda
1 cup all-purpose flour

½ cup chopped walnuts
   or pecans
2½ cups peeled and
   chopped apples
2 tablespoons hot brandy
   (don't let it flame)
1 teaspoon vanilla
Brandy Sauce (below)

Heat oven to 350 degrees. Cream shortening and sugar; add egg and beat. Stir dry ingredients together. Add to creamed mixture and beat thoroughly. Stir in nuts, apples, brandy and vanilla; mix thoroughly.

Pour into greased 8-inch pie pan or 8-or 9-inch round layer pan. Bake for 45-60 minutes. Cool; cut in wedges. Serve with warm Brandy Sauce.

Yield: 8-10 servings.

Variation: Rum or rum flavoring may be substituted for brandy in cake and sauce.

Brandy Sauce:

¾ cup packed brown sugar
½ cup butter

¼ cup half and half cream
1-2 teaspoons brandy

Gently boil brown sugar and butter together for 1 minute. Add cream. Gently boil a few more seconds. Remove from heat and add brandy.

Refrigerate leftover sauce. It will not get sugary when you reheat it.

Yield: 1 cup.

Esther's Tomato Soup Cake
"similar to carrot cake but easier"

1 cup sugar
½ cup shortening
2 eggs, beaten
1 (10¾ oz.) can condensed
    tomato soup
½ teaspoon cinnamon

½ teaspoon cloves
2 teaspoons nutmeg
2 cups all-purpose flour
1 teaspoon baking soda
½ teaspoon salt
1 cup raisins

Heat oven to 350 degrees. Cream sugar and shortening. Add eggs and soup; beat. Add dry ingredients and mix thoroughly. Stir in raisins.
    Pour into greased and floured 13x9x2-inch pan. Bake for 40 minutes. Cool and frost with Cream Cheese Frosting (see Celebration Cake) or other favorite frosting.

Yield: One 13x9-inch cake.

Fruit Torte
"That's right — no shortening!"

¾ cup sugar
1 cup all-purpose flour
1 teaspoon baking soda
¼ teaspoon salt
1 egg, beaten

1 (16 oz.) can fruit cocktail (light
    syrup), drained, or other
    favorite canned fruit
½ cup packed brown sugar
½ cup chopped walnuts or
    pecans

Heat oven to 350 degrees. Mix sugar, flour, baking soda, salt, egg and fruit cocktail. Spread in greased 7x11x2-inch pan. Combine brown sugar and nuts; sprinkle on top. Bake for 45-50 minutes.

Serve warm or cold with whipped cream.

Yield: 8 servings.

Raw Apple Cake
"moist and good"

½ cup margarine, softened
¾ cup sugar
1 egg
½ cup cold coffee
1½ cups all-purpose flour
½ teaspoon cinnamon
¼ teaspoon cloves

¼ teaspoon nutmeg
1 teaspoon baking soda
½ cup raisins
½ cup chopped nuts
½ cup peeled and finely chopped apple (1 large apple)

Heat oven to 350 degrees. Cream margarine and sugar until light and fluffy. Add egg and beat well. Stir in coffee.

Stir dry ingredients together; add to creamed mixture and beat thoroughly. Stir in raisins, nuts and apple.

Pour batter into greased and floured 10-inch bundt pan. Bake for 45 minutes. Cool and cut into ½-1-inch slices.

Yield: One 10-inch bundt cake.

Orange Chocolate Bundt
"definitely do-ahead"

¾ cup butter or margarine, softened
¾ cup sugar
2 eggs
1 teaspoon vanilla
2 tablespoons grated orange peel
¾ cup dairy sour cream
¼ cup water
2½ cups all-purpose flour
1 teaspoon baking soda

1 teaspoon baking powder
1 teaspoon salt
½ pound dates, finely chopped
1 cup chopped walnuts
2 (1 oz.) squares unsweetened chocolate, coarsely grated
½ cup sugar
Juice of 2 oranges (1 cup)
2 tablespoons Grand Marnier (optional)

Heat oven to 325 degrees. Cream butter and ¾ cup sugar until light and fluffy. Add eggs, one at a time, beating thoroughly after each addition. Add vanilla and orange peel.

Combine sour cream and water. Stir dry ingredients together and add alternately with sour cream mixture, beating after each addition. Stir in dates, walnuts and chocolate.

Spoon into greased 10-cup ring mold or 10-inch bundt pan. Bake 1 hour. Cool 10 minutes and place on serving plate.

Heat ½ cup sugar and juice until sugar is dissolved. Simmer slowly

10 minutes. Add Grand Marnier and simmer 2 minutes more.

With bulb baster, drizzle warm orange syrup over warm cake, retrieving syrup and continuing to drizzle onto cake until syrup has been soaked up. This takes about 15 minutes.

The cake should be made a day ahead, covered tightly with plastic wrap and refrigerated. The cake is very rich.

Yield: One 10-inch bundt cake.

Orange-Glazed Pound Cake

"A little fussing, but a special dessert worth the effort."

1 cup butter or margarine	1½ cups all-purpose flour
1 cup sugar	½ cup sugar
4 eggs, separated	¼ cup chopped pecans
1 teaspoon vanilla	½ cup sugar
1 teaspoon orange extract	6 tablespoons orange juice
2½ tablespoons orange juice	Powdered sugar

Heat oven to 350 degrees. Cream butter and 1 cup sugar until light and fluffy. Add egg yolks, one at a time, beating thoroughly after each addition. Mix flavorings with 2½ tablespoons orange juice. Add flour alternately with juice, beating after each addition. Set aside.

Beat egg whites until very soft peaks form. Gradually add ½ cup sugar and beat until stiff but not dry. Gently fold meringue into cake batter.

Sprinkle pecans into bottom of greased 10-inch bundt pan. Carefully turn batter into pan. Bake for 35 to 40 minutes.

Heat ½ cup sugar and 6 tablespoons orange juice to boiling in saucepan. Boil 7 minutes. While cake is warm, pierce with metal skewer; pour half of glaze over cake. Cool cake thoroughly. Glaze again and dust with powdered sugar.

Can be prepared a day ahead.

Yield: One 10-inch bundt cake.

Fruit and Nut Pound Cake

"always brought warm to our family reunions"

3 cups sugar
¼ teaspoon salt
1 cup margarine, softened
½ cup shortening
5 large eggs
1 (5.33 oz.) can evaporated milk
3 cups all-purpose flour

2 teaspoons vanilla butter
   and nut flavor
1 cup chopped nuts
1 cup maraschino cherries,
   drained and halved
1 (8 oz.) jar apricot preserves

Cream sugar, salt, margarine and shortening. Add eggs, one at a time, beating well after each addition.

Add water to evaporated milk to make 1 cup. Add milk and flour to creamed mixture. Beat until thoroughly mixed. Stir flavoring, nuts and cherries into batter.

Pour batter into a greased and floured 10-inch tube pan. Bake at 325 degrees (begin in a cold oven) for 1 hour 45 minutes.

After cake has cooled 5 minutes, remove from pan and spread apricot preserves over hot cake. Serve warm.

Yield: One 10-inch tube cake.

Sweet Lemon-Yogurt Cake

"tastes as good as it sounds"

1 cup butter or margarine,
   softened
1½ cups sugar
6 eggs, separated
2 teaspoons grated lemon peel
1 teaspoon fresh lemon juice or
   ½ teaspoon lemon extract

3 cups cake flour
1 teaspoon baking soda
¼ teaspoon salt
1 cup plain yogurt
2 tablespoons brandy or
   2 tablespoons more yogurt
½ cup sugar

Heat oven to 350 degrees. Cream butter and 1½ cups sugar. Add egg yolks, lemon peel and lemon juice; beat until light and fluffy.

Stir flour, baking soda and salt together; add alternately with yogurt and brandy to creamed mixture, beating after each addition.

Beat egg whites until very soft peaks form; gradually add remaining ½ cup sugar, beating until stiff and glossy. Fold beaten egg whites into batter. Pour into greased 10-inch tube pan or two 9x5x3-inch loaf pans. Bake for 45 minutes. Cool 15 minutes in pan; turn out onto rack.

Cake will keep several days if wrapped well.

Yield: One 10-inch bundt cake or two 9x5x3-inch loaves.

Soft Granola Bars
"nutritious, high-energy snack"

3 cups raisins
½ cup chopped nuts (optional)
⅓ cup honey
1 cup water
¾ cup soy flour
1 cup coarsely ground wheat flour
1½ cups rolled oats

1 teaspoon baking soda
½ teaspoon salt
2 teaspoons cinnamon
½ teaspoon nutmeg
½ teaspoon ground cloves
¾ cup safflower or vegetable oil
1 cup light molasses

In saucepan, combine raisins, nuts, honey and water. Cook over low heat until thick, about 30 minutes.

Heat oven to 400 degrees. Stir dry ingredients together. Add oil and molasses to dry ingredients and mix. Add raisin mixture and mix thoroughly. Pour into greased and floured 13x9x2-inch pan. Bake for 25 to 30 minutes. Cut into bars while still warm.

May be wrapped and frozen.

Yield: 20 (2¼x2½-inch) bars.

Variation: Other dried fruit such as dates, prunes or coarsely chopped apricots can be substituted for raisins.

Eggless Raisin Cake/Bar
"low in cholesterol"

1 cup raisins
2 cups water
½ cup margarine
1 cup sugar
1¾ cups all-purpose flour

1 teaspoon baking soda
½ teaspoon salt
½ teaspoon cinnamon
½ teaspoon nutmeg
½ cup chopped nuts (optional)

In 2-quart saucepan, bring raisins and water to a boil; reduce heat and simmer for 10 minutes. Add margarine and allow to cool.

Heat oven to 350 degrees. Stir dry ingredients together; stir into raisin mixture and mix thoroughly. Stir in nuts.

Pour batter into greased and floured 13x9x2-inch pan. Bake for 35 minutes. Cool and frost with favorite vanilla frosting.

Yield: 12 (3x3-inch) squares or 24 (1½x3-inch) bars.

Fresh Fruit Danish
"endorsed by the family"

3 cups all-purpose flour
½ teaspoon salt (optional)
1 cup shortening
1 egg, separated
Milk
¾ cup corn flake crumbs

¾ cup sugar
1 teaspoon cinnamon
7 cups fresh fruit such as
    apples, pears or peaches,
    peeled and sliced
Vanilla Icing (below)

Heat oven to 375 degrees. Measure flour and salt into large bowl. Cut in shortening until crumbly. Measure egg yolk and add enough milk to make ½ cup. Stir into flour mixture. Divide dough in half.

Roll out ½ of dough to line bottom and sides of 15x10x1-inch jelly roll pan. Sprinkle with corn flake crumbs. Combine sugar and cinnamon; toss with fruit. Arrange fruit slices over crumbs.

Roll out remaining dough; place over fruit and seal edges. Cut vents for steam to escape.

Beat egg white until stiff and brush over pastry. Bake for 1 hour. Drizzle with Vanilla Icing while still warm.

Yield: 32 bars.

Vanilla Icing:

1 cup powdered sugar
3 tablespoons water

1 teaspoon vanilla
Drops of almond flavoring

Mix all ingredients together until smooth.

Yield: ½ cup.

Chewy Delights
"asked for again and again"

⅔ cup sugar
⅔ cup light corn syrup
1 teaspoon vanilla
¾ cup crunchy peanut butter

4½ cups Special K cereal
1 (6 oz.) package butterscotch
    chips
1 (6 oz.) package chocolate chips

In heavy saucepan, bring sugar and syrup to a full boil. Remove from heat. Add vanilla and peanut butter; blend well. Stir in cereal.

Press mixture firmly into 13x9x2-inch buttered pan. Melt chips together over hot water and spread on bars. Cool; cut into squares.

Yield: 24 squares.

Puffed Rice Bars

"crunchy good"

¼ cup margarine
1 cup sugar
¼ teaspoon salt
1 cup peanuts

5½ cups puffed rice cereal
(not Rice Krispies)
2 tablespoons toasted sesame
seeds

Melt margarine in 4-quart heavy saucepan. Add sugar and salt; cook over medium high heat, stirring constantly until a light golden color. Margarine will not completely absorb into caramelized mixture.

Add peanuts and puffed rice; stir quickly. Add sesame seeds and continue stirring until all rice is uniformly coated.

Turn into greased 11x7x1-inch pan, packing mixture down firmly with a greased cup. Cool; cut into very small bars and store in air-tight container.

Yield: 50 bars.

Pecan Bars

"as good as pecan pie"

1 cup butter, softened
2 cups all-purpose flour
¾ cup packed brown sugar
5 eggs

¾ cup granulated sugar
1 cup light corn syrup
1 teaspoon vanilla
1 cup pecan halves

Heat oven to 350 degrees. Mix butter, flour and brown sugar together. Pat dough into 13x9x2-inch pan. Bake for 12 minutes.

Beat eggs. Add remaining ingredients; mix thoroughly. Pour over baked crust. Bake for 15 minutes. Lower heat to 275 degrees and continue baking for 30 minutes more or until set. Cool; cut into bars.

Freezes well.

Yield: 36 (2x2-inch) bars.

Mint Stick Brownies

"rich and minty for a special treat"

2 (1 oz.) squares unsweetened
   chocolate
½ cup butter
1 cup sugar
2 eggs, well beaten
½ cup all-purpose flour
¼ teaspoon baking powder

⅛ teaspoon salt
¼ teaspoon peppermint extract
½ cup chopped nuts
Peppermint Frosting (below)
1 (1 oz.) square unsweetened
   chocolate
1 tablespoon butter

Heat oven to 350 degrees. Melt 2 squares chocolate and ½ cup butter in top of double boiler. Add sugar and beaten eggs.

Stir flour, baking powder and salt together. Add to chocolate mixture. When well mixed, add peppermint extract and nuts. Pour into ungreased 9x9x2-inch pan. Bake for 25 minutes. Cool and spread with Peppermint Frosting.

When set, melt 1 square chocolate and 1 tablespoon butter together; drizzle over frosting. Refrigerate to set. Cut into bars.

Yield: 36 bars.

Peppermint Frosting:

2 tablespoons butter, softened
1 cup powdered sugar
1 tablespoon whipping cream

½ teaspoon peppermint extract
Green food coloring

Beat butter, powdered sugar, cream and extract together until smooth and fluffy. Add food coloring a drop at a time until desired color is reached.

Yield: about ½ cup.

DESSERTS

Fresh Fruit and Yogurt

"Fresh yogurt takes the place of whipped cream for people who value their slim waistlines."

2 cups fresh strawberries,
   raspberries or sliced peaches
½ cup plain yogurt

3 tablespoons honey
1 teaspoon finely grated
   lemon peel

Place strawberries, raspberries or peaches in individual dessert dishes. Spoon 2 tablespoons of yogurt on top of fruit. Drizzle honey over yogurt; sprinkle with lemon peel.

Yield: 4 servings.

Cheese and Fruit with Raspberry Yogurt Dressing

"pineapple, plums, melons, what have you"

1 large pineapple
¼ watermelon
1 cantaloupe
3 bananas

1 pound plums
1 pound seedless green grapes
Raspberry Yogurt Dressing (below)

Peel, remove seeds or core and cut fruit into bite-size pieces.
   Select assorted cheeses such as: Stilton or blue cheese, havarti, gourmandaise, Cheddar and gouda.
   Arrange fruit and cheese attractively in separate piles on large platter. Serve with Raspberry Yogurt Dressing.

Yield: 12-14 servings.

Raspberry Yogurt Dressing:

1 cup yogurt
2 tablespoons honey

½ cup fresh mashed raspberries
   put through a sieve

Combine all ingredients; cover and refrigerate.

Yield: 1½ cups.

Gingered Melon
"veto-proof"

1 large honeydew melon
1 large cantaloupe

¼ cup powdered sugar
1 teaspoon ground ginger

Peel melons and cut into small pieces. Combine sugar and ginger; sprinkle over melons. Toss; refrigerate 1 hour. Alternate melon cubes on bamboo skewers.

Yield: about 16 skewers.

Lemony Tokay and Melon Compote
"simple and superb"

3 cups cantaloupe cubes
2 cups halved and seeded Tokay grapes
1 (3 oz.) package cream cheese, softened

¼ cup sugar
3 tablespoons milk
1 cup lemon yogurt
Chopped nuts

Combine fruits; chill.
Beat cream cheese with sugar and milk until fluffly; fold in yogurt. Spoon over fruit in individual dishes. Garnish with chopped nuts.

Yield: 6 servings.

Light, Quick and Yummy
"the title says it all"

2 oranges, peeled and sliced
2 bananas, sliced lengthwise
½ cup raisins
1 cup dairy sour cream

1 teaspoon vanilla
2 tablespoons brown sugar
2 tablespoons slivered almonds

Combine oranges and bananas in oven-proof dish. Sprinkle with raisins.
Combine sour cream and vanilla; spread over fruits. Sprinkle with brown sugar and almonds. Broil until sugar dissolves. Watch carefully to avoid burning.

Yield: 4 servings.

Fruit Slush

"Refreshing for brunch, a snack or a dessert."

3 medium bananas
½ cup sugar
1 (12 oz.) can frozen orange juice
   concentrate, thawed

1 (16 oz.) bottle ginger ale or 7-up
1 (20 oz.) can crushed pineapple,
   undrained

Mash bananas; add sugar and mix well. Mix in remaining ingredients.
Turn mixture into a 9x9x2-inch pan or equivalent size plastic container.
Freeze until firm.

Before serving, let stand at room temperature for about 45 minutes
or thaw in microwave until slushy.

Yield: 10 servings.

Pineapple-Orange Sherbet

"Easy, my kind of cooking!"

1 (46 oz.) can orange juice
1 (46 oz.) can pineapple juice

Pour orange juice into ice cube trays and freeze until solid. Remove
from freezer and separate cubes.

Pour 2½ cups pineapple juice in blender. Blend on medium speed.
Add frozen orange juice cubes one at a time until mixture becomes
thick and frothy. Spoon into sherbet glasses.

Repeat with remaining pineapple juice and orange juice cubes. Store
in freezer until time to serve.

Yield: 8 servings.

Seward's Folly

"lemon-sweet frozen dessert"

2 cups vanilla wafer crumbs
3 large eggs, separated
½ cup sugar

5 tablespoons fresh lemon juice
1 cup whipping cream
1½ teaspoons grated lemon peel

Line an ice cube tray with waxed paper, having ends of paper
extend over sides for easy removal. Press crumbs into bottom of tray,
reserving 2 tablespoons.

Beat egg whites, gradually adding sugar, until stiff peaks form. Beat
egg yolks until thick and lemon-colored. Add lemon juice to cream and

beat until cream holds soft peaks. Fold egg yolks into egg whites; fold eggs into cream. Fold in lemon peel and pour into paper-lined tray. Sprinkle reserved crumbs on top.

Freeze 6 hours or overnight. Remove from freezer and transfer to refrigerator ½ hour before serving. Cut into slices and serve immediately.

Yield: 6-8 servings.

Winter Berry Parfaits
"Freeze a bag of cranberries in the fall and surprise summer guests."

2 cups whole cranberries	**1 cup sugar**
1 cinnamon stick	**Pinch of salt**
1 cup water	**1 quart vanilla ice cream**

In 2-quart saucepan, bring cranberries, cinnamon stick and water to a boil. Lower heat, cover and simmer 5 minutes. Add sugar and salt; cook uncovered 2 minutes to dissolve sugar. Cool; remove cinnamon.

Alternate layers of ice cream and sauce in parfait glasses.

Can be prepared ahead and kept frozen until serving time.

Yield: 6 servings.

Strawberries Romanoff
"a summer favorite"

2 quarts fresh strawberries	**Juice of ½ medium lemon**
1 cup whipping cream	**1 tablespoon Cointreau**
1 pint French vanilla ice cream, softened	**1 tablespoon rum**

Wash strawberries; reserve 8-10 for garnish. Hull remaining berries, sprinkle with sugar and refrigerate.

Whip cream and combine with ice cream. Add lemon juice, Cointreau and rum. Pour over strawberries. Garnish each serving with a whole strawberry.

Yield: 8-10 servings.

Blueberry Dessert
"blueberries remembered in the winter"

12 graham crackers	2 tablespoons cornstarch
¼ cup granulated sugar	½ cup granulated sugar
½ cup butter, melted	½ cup water
2 eggs, beaten	2½ cups fresh or frozen
1 teaspoon vanilla	blueberries
1 (8 oz.) package cream cheese, softened	½ teaspoon lemon juice
	1 cup whipping cream, whipped
½ cup powdered sugar	

Heat oven to 375 degrees. Crush graham crackers; mix with ¼ cup granulated sugar and butter. Press gently into 8x8x2- or 9x9x2-inch pan.

Combine eggs, vanilla, cream cheese and powdered sugar; beat until creamy. Pour over graham cracker crust. Bake for 15 minutes.

In saucepan, mix cornstarch and ½ cup granulated sugar; stir in water. Add blueberries; cook and stir until thick. Stir in lemon juice. Cool slightly; pour over cream cheese. Refrigerate until chilled. Serve topped with whipped cream.

Yield: 8-9 servings.

Variation: For the additional tanginess of fresh blueberries, fold 1 extra cup fresh blueberries into cooked blueberry mixture just before pouring over cream cheese.

Hopkins Raspberry Tart
"for the Fourth of July"

2 tablespoons sugar	2 tablespoons flour
1 cup all-purpose flour	¼ teaspoon cinnamon
½ cup butter or margarine	4 cups fresh raspberries
1 tablespoon vinegar	

Heat oven to 375 degrees. Stir sugar into 1 cup flour; cut in butter with pastry blender; stir in vinegar. Pat dough onto bottom and 1 inch up side of 10-inch loose-bottom French tart pan or springform pan.

Mix 2 tablespoons flour and cinnamon; toss with 3 cups raspberries and pour into crust. Bake for about 1 hour. Remove from oven and spread 1 cup raspberries on top. Cool, remove rim and serve.

Yield: 8 servings.

Variation: Fresh blueberries may be substituted for the raspberries.

Sherry Trifle
"final testimony to a marvelous dinner"

1 (10¾ oz.) baked pound cake
1 (5¾ oz.) package vanilla
  pudding and pie filling mix
  (not instant)
2 cups half and half cream
2 (10 oz.) packages frozen
  raspberries

1 (10 oz.) package frozen peaches
  in syrup
¼ cup semi-dry sherry
2 cups whipping cream
¼ cup powdered sugar

Cut pound cake into ½-inch slices. Make pudding according to package directions, except use 2 cups cream instead of 3 cups milk.

In an attractive bowl, about 10 inches in diameter, layer half of pound cake, half of pudding, half of raspberries and half of peaches; sprinkle with 2 tablespoons sherry. Repeat layers. Cover and refrigerate at least 8 hours.

Just before serving, whip cream with powdered sugar. Spread over trifle.

Yield: 6-8 servings.

Chocolate Mousse Crown
"Calorie counters — don't even read this recipe!"

16 ladyfingers
½ cup dry sherry
1 cup semisweet chocolate chips
2 (8 oz.) packages cream cheese,
  softened
¾ cup packed brown sugar

¼ teaspoon salt
4 eggs, separated
2 teaspoons vanilla
¾ cup packed brown sugar
2 cups whipping cream, whipped

Split ladyfingers lengthwise and place cut side down on cookie sheet. Bake at 375 degrees for 5 minutes. Cool about 10 minutes; brush cut side with sherry. Place about 24 pieces around side of 10-inch springform pan. Arrange remaining pieces on bottom.

Melt chocolate chips over simmering water. Cool 10 minutes.

Blend cream cheese, ¾ cup brown sugar and salt. Beat in egg yolks one at a time, beating well after each addition. Stir in cooled chocolate. Beat egg whites and vanilla until very soft peaks form. Gradually add ¾ cup brown sugar while beating egg whites. Beat until stiff peaks form. Fold egg whites and whipped cream into chocolate mixture; pour into prepared pan. Refrigerate 5 hours or overnight.

Yield: 20 servings.

Chocolate Shell Amaretto Cheesecake
"straw vote winner"

1 (3½ oz.) package blanched almonds, chopped and toasted
1 tablespoon butter
1 (8 oz.) package chocolate wafer cookies, finely crushed
¼ cup sugar
6 tablespoons butter, softened
1 cup sugar

3 (8 oz.) packages cream cheese, softened
3 jumbo eggs
⅓ cup whipping cream
¼ cup amaretto
1 teaspoon vanilla
1 (16 oz.) carton dairy sour cream
1 tablespoon sugar
1 teaspoon vanilla

Sauté almonds in 1 tablespoon butter. Combine almonds, chocolate wafer crumbs, ¼ cup sugar and 6 tablespoons butter until well mixed. Press onto bottom and up side of buttered 9-inch springform pan.

Heat oven to 375 degrees. Cream 1 cup sugar and cream cheese together; beat in eggs, one at a time. Beat until creamy and well-mixed. Add whipping cream, amaretto and 1 teaspoon vanilla. Beat until light and fluffy. Pour into springform pan. Bake on middle shelf of oven for 45 minutes.

Cool on wire rack and let stand for 15 minutes. (Cheesecake will not be set in the center.)

Combine sour cream, 1 tablespoon sugar and 1 teaspoon vanilla. Spread evenly over cheesecake and return to oven for an additional 15 minutes. Cool cake completely on wire rack. Cover lightly and refrigerate several hours or overnight.

Yield: 12-16 servings.

Win-Them-Over Cheesecake
"a membership booster"

1 cup graham cracker crumbs
½ cup finely chopped walnuts
⅓ cup butter or margarine, softened
3 (8 oz.) packages cream cheese, softened

1½ cups sugar
6 eggs
1 (16 oz.) carton dairy sour cream
2 tablespoons cornstarch
1 tablespoon fresh lemon juice
2 teaspoons vanilla

Heat oven to 350 degrees. Mix graham cracker crumbs, walnuts and butter with a fork. Press firmly on bottom and 1½ inches up side of 9-inch springform pan.

Beat cream cheese until smooth. Gradually beat in sugar; add eggs, one at a time; add sour cream, cornstarch, lemon juice and vanilla, blending on low speed. Beat at medium speed for 3 minutes.

Pour into springform pan and bake for 1 hour or until lightly browned. Turn off oven; let cheesecake remain in oven another 30 minutes. Remove from oven; cool in pan on wire rack. Cover and refrigerate.

Fruits — frozen or fresh — of all kinds may be used to top or garnish cheesecake. Other garnishing variations include: toasted, slivered or whole nuts in combination with fruit or alone; toasted coconut chips or slivers; candied shredded citrus fruit peels; shaved, grated, bitter or semisweet chocolate; chocolate curls; fruit glazes and various preserves.

Yield: 12 to 16 servings.

Holiday Rum Pudding

"beautiful for a holiday meal"

1 envelope unflavored gelatin	½ cup light rum
¼ cup cold water	Dash of salt
5 egg yolks	1 cup whipping cream, whipped
⅔ cup sugar	Lingonberry Sauce (below)
2 cups hot milk	

Combine gelatin and cold water. Beat egg yolks with sugar until thick and lemon-colored. Slowly add hot milk, stirring constantly. Pour into top of double boiler and cook over simmering water, stirring constantly, until thick and will coat a metal spoon. Add gelatin, stirring until fully dissolved. Cool.

Fold in rum, salt and whipped cream. Turn into individual molds or 6-cup mold. Refrigerate until set.

Unmold on platter and garnish with a bit of sauce and sprig of holly, serving remainder of sauce in a side dish.

Yield: 8-10 servings.

Lingonberry Sauce:

1 (12 oz.) carton fresh lingonberries	½ cup water
	1 cup sugar

Drain lingonberries. Rinse several times with cold water; drain.

Place berries in saucepan with ½ cup water. Simmer slowly 15 minutes. Add sugar and bring to a boil, stirring constantly. Cool and serve over pudding.

Yield: 1½-2 cups.

Tortoni

"elegant — and can be served from your freezer"

2 cups whipping cream
½ cup powdered sugar
2 egg whites

1 cup crushed Italian macaroons
(about 12)
1 tablespoon dry Marsala or
sherry

Whip cream until it forms a ribbon, not peaks; beat in powdered sugar. Beat egg whites until stiff but not dry. Set aside ¼ cup macaroons. Fold remaining macaroons into whipped cream. Fold in Marsala, then egg whites.

Pour into dessert dishes, ramekins or paper cups. Sprinkle with reserved macaroons. Freeze.

Yield: 8 servings.

Orange Marmalade Soufflé

"stove-top soufflé"

3 egg whites
3 tablespoons sugar

1 tablespoon orange marmalade
Custard Sauce (below)

Beat egg whites until very soft peaks form. Add sugar, a little at a time, and continue beating until stiff peaks form. Beat in orange marmalade.

Immediately put into top of lightly buttered 1½-quart double boiler. Place over simmering water, cover tightly and let cook until soufflé is set, at least 1 hour. (Soufflé will hold up to 2 hours.)

Carefully invert onto serving platter or spoon out individual servings into dishes.

Serve with Custard Sauce, a dab of orange marmalade or whipped cream, if desired.

Yield: 3-4 servings.

Custard Sauce:

2 cups milk
4 egg yolks, slightly beaten
¼ cup sugar

⅛ teaspoon salt
1 teaspoon vanilla

Heat milk in top of double boiler. Slowly stir in egg yolks, sugar and salt. Cook over simmering water, stirring constantly, until custard coats a metal spoon. Let cool; add vanilla.

Yield: about 3 cups.

Election Confection
"no-bake mint dessert"

1 cup chopped walnuts or pecans	4 eggs
2 (1 oz.) squares unsweetened chocolate	½ teaspoon peppermint extract
	2 teaspoons vanilla
1 cup butter or margarine	½ cup chopped walnuts or pecans
2 cups powdered sugar	

Divide 1 cup nuts evenly among small ramekins or foil baking cups.

Melt chocolate in top of double boiler over simmering water; cool. In large mixer bowl, beat butter and powdered sugar until fluffy. Add chocolate and beat thoroughly. Add eggs, one at a time, beating 1-2 minutes after each addition. Add peppermint and vanilla.

Spoon into ramekins; sprinkle with ½ cup nuts. Refrigerate or freeze.

Yield: 18 servings.

Forgotten Meringue Cake
"a lemon-light ending for an unforgetable meal"

6 egg whites	¼ teaspoon salt
¼ teaspoon cream of tartar	1½ cups sugar
1 teaspoon vanilla	Lemon Filling (below)

Heat oven to 450 degrees. Beat egg whites until frothy. Add cream of tartar, vanilla and salt; beat until very soft peaks form. Add sugar, 2 tablespoons at a time, continuing to beat until stiff peaks form.

Spread in greased 10x6x2-inch pan. Put meringue in oven; turn off oven and leave meringue in oven overnight.

Spread Lemon Filling over meringue. Refrigerate. Cut in squares to serve.

Yield: 6-9 servings.

Lemon Filling:

6 egg yolks	¾ cup sugar
¼ cup fresh lemon juice	½ cup whipping cream, whipped
3 tablespoons water	

Combine egg yolks, lemon juice, water and sugar in saucepan. Cook until thick. Cool; fold in whipped cream.

Yield: about 2½ cups.

Unimpeachable Cobbler
"beyond reproach"

½ cup butter or margarine
1 cup sugar
1 cup all-purpose flour
2 teaspoons baking powder

¼ teaspoon salt
¾ cup milk
5 cups fresh peach slices
  or 16 oz. frozen peach slices,
  thawed and drained

Heat oven to 350 degrees. Melt butter in 13x9x2-inch pan. Mix sugar, flour, baking powder, salt and milk together; pour into pan. Arrange peach slices on top. Bake for 60 minutes until golden brown and crunchy.

Yield: 8-10 servings.

Steamed Cranberry Pudding
"robust and warming"

3 cups raw cranberries
¾ cup raisins
2¼ cups all-purpose flour
3 teaspoons baking soda

¾ cup light molasses
½ cup hot water
Butter Cream Sauce (below)

Wash cranberries; drain. Combine cranberries and raisins in large mixing bowl. Stir flour and soda together and sprinkle over fruit.

Add molasses and hot water; stir until well mixed. Pour into two 1-pound greased, lightly-sugared coffee cans. Cover ends with foil.

Place on rack in deep kettle. Add enough boiling water to come halfway up sides of cans. Steam covered for 1¼ hours.

Serve warm with warm Butter Cream Sauce.

To prepare in advance, cool puddings on a wire rack, wrap in foil and refrigerate or freeze. To serve, bake at 325 degrees for 45 minutes or until hot.

Yield: 12-14 servings (2 pudding molds).

Butter Cream Sauce:

1 cup sugar
½ cup butter

½ cup light cream
1 teaspoon vanilla.

Combine ingredients and heat to boiling over moderate heat.

Yield: 1½ cups (for 1 pudding mold).

Baked Chocolate Pudding
"a chocoholic's choice"

1 cup all-purpose flour	½ cup chopped nuts
¼ teaspoon salt	1 teaspoon vanilla
¾ cup granulated sugar	½ cup granulated sugar
2 teaspoons baking powder	½ cup packed brown sugar
1½ tablespoons cocoa	5 teaspoons cocoa
½ cup milk	1 cup water
2 tablespoons butter, melted	

Heat oven to 325 degrees. Stir together flour, salt, ¾ cup granulated sugar, baking powder and 1½ tablespoons cocoa. Add milk, butter, nuts and vanilla; mix well. Pour into greased 8x8x2 or 7x11x2-inch pan.

Combine remaining ingredients; pour over mixture in pan. Bake for 1 hour.

Serve warm or cold with a dollop of whipped or ice cream, if desired.

Yield: 9 servings.

Deep Dish Apples
"a Minnesota miracle"

8 large tart apples, peeled, cored and sliced	¼ cup butter
	Pastry for 9-inch one crust pie
¾-1 cup sugar	¼ cup rum
Juice and grated peel of 1 orange	

Heat oven to 450 degrees. Place apples in deep casserole dish. Sprinkle apples with sugar, juice and peel. Dot with butter.

Roll out pastry ⅛ inch thick. Cut a small round vent hole in center of pastry. Place pastry over top of casserole, sealing edge of pastry to edge of casserole.

Bake for 15 minutes. Reduce oven temperature to 350 degrees and continue baking for 45 minutes or until crust is golden and apples are tender.

Remove casserole from oven and pour rum through the hole in the crust. Serve warm in sauce dishes with whipping cream, unwhipped.

Yield: 6-8 servings.

Fresh Peach Pie
"Splurge!"

1 cup sugar
1 cup water
2 tablespoons cornstarch
1 (3-oz.) package peach-flavored
gelatin

6 medium size fresh peaches
9-inch baked pie shell
Whipped cream

In 1-quart saucepan, combine sugar, water and cornstarch; cook over medium heat until clear and thick, stirring constantly. Stir in gelatin; cool.

Peel and slice peaches and put in pie shell. Pour gelatin mixture over peaches. Refrigerate until set. Garnish with whipped cream.

Yield: 6-8 servings.

Variation: Other fresh fruits such as sliced bananas and fresh or frozen blueberries can be added with peaches. Fully ripe nectarines can be substituted for peaches.

Coffeescotch Pie
"an unlikely combination that works well"

⅓ cup chunky peanut butter
⅔ cup powdered sugar
9-inch baked pie shell
1 (3⅝ oz.) package butterscotch
pudding and pie filling mix
(not instant)

2 teaspoons instant coffee
1 (13 oz.) can evaporated milk
½ cup water
2 eggs, separated
¼ teaspoon cream of tartar
¼ cup granulated sugar

With fork or pastry blender, cut peanut butter into sugar until it looks like coarse crumbs. Spread all but 1 tablespoon in pie shell.

In saucepan, combine pudding mix, instant coffee, milk, water and egg yolks. Stir and cook over medium heat to a full boil. Cool 5 minutes; spoon into pie shell.

Heat oven to 425 degrees. Beat egg whites and cream of tartar until very soft peaks form. Gradually add ¼ cup sugar, beating until stiff glossy peaks form. Spread over filling. Sprinkle with reserved crumbs.

Bake 5-8 minutes or until meringue is golden brown. Cool to room temperature.

Yield: 8 servings.

Praline Pumpkin Pie

"the party's ticket to success"

1 envelope unflavored gelatin	¾ teaspoon nutmeg
½ cup cold water	¼ cup milk
¾ cup packed brown sugar	1 cup whipping cream, whipped
1 (16 oz.) can pumpkin	Praline Crunch (below)
½ teaspoon salt	9-inch baked pie shell
1 teaspoon cinnamon	Whipped cream

Sprinkle gelatin over water in saucepan. Place over low heat, stirring constantly until gelatin is dissolved, 2-3 minutes. Remove from heat; add brown sugar and stir until dissolved.

In a large mixing bowl, combine pumpkin, salt, cinnamon and nutmeg. Add milk and mix thoroughly. Gradually add gelatin mixture to pumpkin mixture, stirring until smooth. Fold whipped cream into pumpkin mixture.

Sprinkle 1 cup Praline Crunch over bottom of baked pie shell. Pour pumpkin mixture into pie shell. Refrigerate several hours until firm.

Just before serving, garnish with whipped cream and remaining Praline Crunch.

Yield: 6-8 servings.

Praline Crunch:

¼ cup butter or margarine	1 cup coarsely chopped pecans
½ cup sugar	

Melt butter in small skillet; stir in sugar. Add pecans; cook over moderate heat, stirring constantly until sugar mixture begins to turn golden, about 3 minutes.

Remove from heat and turn out onto aluminum foil or greased jelly roll pan. Cool; break into small pieces.

Yield: 1½ cups.

Fresh Blueberry Pie
"my best"

1 cup fresh blueberries	¼ cup slivered almonds
¾ cup sugar	1 tablespoon Cointreau
½ cup water	3 cups fresh blueberries
2 tablespoons cornstarch	9-inch baked pie shell
3 tablespoons water	Crème Chantilly (below)
1 tablespoon butter	

Combine 1 cup blueberries, sugar and ½ cup water in saucepan. Bring to a boil and simmer until soft. Rub through a sieve or purée in blender or food processor.

Dissolve cornstarch in 3 tablespoons water and add to purée, bring to a boil and boil 1 minute.

Sauté almonds in butter and add to purée. Fold Cointreau and 3 cups blueberries into purée; pour into pie shell. Refrigerate for several hours. Serve topped with Crème Chantilly.

Yield: 8-10 servings.

Crème Chantilly:

2 tablespoons sugar	1 cup whipping cream, whipped
¼ teaspoon almond extract	

Gently stir sugar and almond extract into whipped cream.

Yield: about 2 cups.

Arboretum Peach Pie

"take along for a picnic"

Filling:

¼ cup butter or margarine, softened
¼ cup sugar
2 tablespoons flour
½ cup light corn syrup

¼ teaspoon salt
3 eggs
2 cups peeled, diced fresh peaches

10-inch unbaked pie shell

Topping:

¼ cup flour
2 tablespoons butter or margarine, softened

¼ cup packed brown sugar
½ cup coarsely chopped pecans

Heat oven to 400 degrees. Cream together butter, sugar and flour. Beat in syrup and salt. Add eggs, one at a time, beating well after each. Stir in peaches. Pour into pie shell.

Combine topping ingredients, except pecans, with fork or pastry blender. Stir in pecans. Sprinkle topping over filling. Bake 35 minutes or until knife inserted in center comes out clean. Refrigerate until serving.

Yield: 8 servings.

Upside-Down Pecan-Apple Pie

"Mom was a creative cook."

2 tablespoons butter
¼ cup pecan halves
⅓ cup packed brown sugar

Pastry for 2-crust pie
Filling for favorite apple pie

Heat oven to 400 degrees. Fit a 13-inch circle of aluminum foil into a 9-inch pie pan; press down. Spread with butter. Arrange pecan halves in circles covering bottom of pan. Pat brown sugar over nuts.

Put pie crust over nuts. Fill with apple pie filling. Put on top crust; seal edge. Bake for 15 minutes; lower oven temperature to 350 degrees and bake 35-40 minutes longer, until juices bubble.

Remove pie from oven and invert on large serving platter. The sides will collapse a little as the pie cools.

Yield: 8 servings.

Prince of Wales Pie

"a Duluth specialty"

¾ cup packed brown sugar
¾ cup butter
1 (14 oz.) can sweetened
   condensed milk

½ cup chopped walnuts
⅓ cup raisins
9-inch baked pie shell
Whipped cream

Place brown sugar, butter and sweetened condensed milk in saucepan over medium heat. Bring to a boil; cook and stir about 7 minutes to thicken.

Remove from heat. Stir in walnuts and raisins. Pour into pie shell; cool. Serve with whipped cream.

Yield: 10 servings.

Peanut Butter Sauce

"Take affirmative action — reform tomorrow!"

1½ cups sugar
1 tablespoon cocoa
1 cup water

2 cups marshmallow creme
2 cups peanut butter
1 cup light corn syrup

Mix sugar and cocoa in heavy saucepan. Add water and bring to a boil, cooking for 5 minutes. Remove from heat and beat in marshmallow creme, peanut butter and corn syrup. Serve over ice cream.

Yield: about 7 cups.

Granola
"less honey and oil than commercial varieties"

6 cups thick rolled oats*
2 cups rolled wheat*
1 cup wheat germ
½ cup raw sesame seeds
½ cup raw sunflower nuts
½ cup non-instant dry milk*

1 teaspoon cinnamon
½ teaspoon nutmeg
½ cup honey or maple syrup
½ cup vegetable oil
¾ cup raisins

Put rolled oats and rolled wheat in 13x9x2-inch pan or large broiler pan. Bake at 250 degrees for 15 minutes.

In 4-quart bowl, mix wheat germ, sesame seeds, sunflower nuts, dry milk, cinnamon and nutmeg. Stir in warmed oats and wheat. Stir in honey and oil; mix until all is moistened.

Bake at 250 degrees 30-35 minutes, stirring every 10 minutes. Bake for 45 minutes if a toastier taste is desired. Cool. Stir in raisins.

*Available at a co-op or health food store.
This recipe is high in complex carbohydrates and low in fats and simple sugars.

Yield: 3-pound coffee can full.

Variations: Add ½ cup coconut, ½ cup almonds or filberts; other dried fruit. Rolled rye can be substituted for part of the rolled oats or rolled wheat.

English Toffee
"butterscotch candy combined with chocolate and nuts"

2 cups sugar
½ cup water
¼ cup light corn syrup
1 cup butter or margarine

10 ounces semisweet chocolate candy bars, chopped or grated, or chocolate chips
1 cup finely chopped walnuts

Combine sugar, water, corn syrup and butter in heavy skillet. Cook over medium heat, stirring frequently to hard crack stage (300 degrees). Syrup will be thick and amber-colored. Watch carefully to avoid burning.

Pour into buttered 15x10x1-inch pan. Spread evenly; cool slightly. Sprinkle grated chocolate over candy. As chocolate melts, spread evenly. Sprinkle nuts on top and pat into softened chocolate. When candy has cooled, break into pieces.

Yield: 1 pound.

Election Night Caramel Corn

"make a batch while waiting for the returns"

8 quarts popped corn
2 cups packed brown sugar
½ cup light corn syrup
½ cup butter

½ teaspoon baking soda
Pinch of cream of tartar
Dash of salt

Put popped corn in large roasting pan. Mix brown sugar, syrup and butter in heavy saucepan. Bring to a boil and cook 5 minutes. Remove from heat; add baking soda, cream of tartar and salt; stir. Immediately pour hot syrup over popped corn; mix thoroughly.

Bake at 200 degrees for 1 hour. Place hot caramel corn on waxed paper and separate into bite-size pieces.

Yield: 8 quarts.

Kickoff Popcorn

"after-school fortification"

18 cups unsalted popped corn
½ cup margarine or butter
2 tablespoons Worcestershire
   sauce

¼ teaspoon Tabasco sauce
½ teaspoon garlic salt
½ teaspoon onion salt

Put popcorn in large roasting pan. Melt margarine, stir in spices; pour over popcorn. Bake at 250 degrees for 1 hour, stirring every 15 minutes. Cool and store in airtight container.

Yield: 10 servings (4½ quarts).

Caramels
"for a broad-based constituency"

2 cups sugar
1¾ cups light corn syrup
1 cup butter

1 (13 oz.) can evaporated milk
1½ teaspoons vanilla

Place sugar, corn syrup, butter and milk in 4-quart saucepan on high heat for 5 minutes. Lower heat to medium when butter has melted and continue cooking, stirring constantly, until mixture reaches firm ball stage (246 degrees), about 40 minutes.

Remove from heat and add vanilla. Pour into buttered 13x9x2-inch pan. Cool thoroughly. Turn out onto plexiglas or wooden board and cut into squares; a pizza cutter works well. Wrap each square in waxed paper.

Yield: about 10 dozen.

Grandma Hall's Candied Pecans
"These will keep for many months refrigerated in a tight container."

1 pound pecan halves
2 egg whites
¾ cup sugar

pinch of salt
½ cup butter or margarine

Spread pecans in jelly roll pan. Heat in oven at 300 degrees for 10 minutes. Beat egg whites, sugar and salt until soft peaks form. Toss nuts in egg white mixture to coat.

Melt butter on jelly roll pan in oven. Spread coated nuts on melted butter in pan.

Bake at 325 degrees for 30 minutes, stirring every 10 minutes.

Yield: 1 pound.

Buttery Cashew Brittle
"a deliciously different version"

2 cups sugar
1 cup light corn syrup
½ cup water

1 cup butter
3 cups (12 oz.) cashews
1 teaspoon baking soda

In 3-quart saucepan, combine sugar, corn syrup and water. Cook and stir until sugar dissolves. Bring to a boil and stir in butter. Stir frequently after mixture reaches thread stage (230 degrees).

Add cashews when temperature reaches soft crack stage (280 degrees). Stir constantly until it reaches hard crack stage (300 degrees). Remove from heat and quickly stir in baking soda. Mix thoroughly. Pour into 2 buttered 15x10x1-inch pans, spreading as thin as possible. Let rest 3-4 minutes. Put on aluminum foil and pull quickly until thin. Let cool. Break into bite-size pieces.

Yield: 2½ pounds.

Vice President's Brandy Pot

"store in a cool, dark place"

1 quart perfect ripe strawberries, washed and hulled
1 quart sugar
2 cups brandy
1 pint Bing cherries, washed and stemmed
1 pint sugar

1 pint fresh pineapple chunks
1 pint sugar
1 pint blueberries
1 pint sugar
1 pint peaches, sliced
1 pint sugar

Place strawberries and 1 quart sugar in a half-gallon or one-gallon stone or Mason-type jar with tight-fitting lid. Let stand about an hour. Cover with brandy. Cover tightly, clamping if possible. If using aluminum foil, place weighted plate on top. Store in dark place if using glass so that fruit will not discolor.

When cherries become available, let stand overnight with sugar. Add with syrup to jar.

Add pineapple, blueberries, peaches or other soft-skinned fruits with equal parts sugar as the fruits come on the market. Very soft-skinned fruits, like bananas or melons, and tough-skinned fruits, like grapes and apples, do not brandy well.

Add the last fruit around September, then seal the jar well. Open just before Christmas. The fruit will be dark and mellow. Pack in clean pint jars for holiday gifts.

Serve as accompaniment for meat and as a delicious rich sauce over ice cream, pudding or chiffon-type pies.

Yield: Variable, depending upon quantity of fruits used.

Zucchini Jam
"a dark horse winner"

6 small or 2 medium zucchini
6 cups sugar
½ cup lemon juice

1 (8 oz.) can crushed pineapple
1 (3 oz.) package apricot-flavored gelatin

Peel and shred zucchini to make 6 cups, well-packed; let stand 1 hour in collander to drain.

Put zucchini in large kettle over medium heat; watch carefully. When it starts to boil, boil 6 minutes or until clear. Add sugar, lemon juice, pineapple and its juice. Return to a boil and boil 6 minutes. Take off heat and add apricot gelatin. Stir well.

Ladle into hot sterilized jars; seal.

If using large zucchini, remove all seeds before shredding.

Yield: 6 pints.

Green Pepper Jelly
"excellent on cheese and crackers"

1 cup finely chopped green
   pepper
¾ cup white wine vinegar
1 clove garlic, crushed (optional)

¾ cup water
5 cups sugar
1 (3 oz.) package liquid pectin
Few drops green food coloring

Bring green pepper, vinegar, garlic and water to a boil. Add sugar and pectin; return to boiling. Boil about 1 minute. Remove from heat; skim off foam. Add food coloring.

Pour into hot sterilized jars; seal with lids or paraffin.

Yield: 7 (8 oz.) jars.

Harvest Time Tangerine Relish
"serve with turkey, pork or ham"

1 pound fresh or frozen
   cranberries
2 cups sugar
1 cup water
1 (2½-inch) cinnamon stick

2 medium apples, pared and
   thinly sliced
Grated peel of 1 lemon
Grated peel of 2 tangerines
3 tangerines, peeled, sectioned
   and seeded

Wash and pick over cranberries; drain. Place in large saucepan with remaining ingredients, except tangerine segments. Bring to a boil, stirring occasionally. Reduce heat and simmer 5-7 minutes or until cranberry skins pop and apples are transparent.

Transfer to glass bowl. Gently stir in tangerine segments. Refrigerate several hours or until icy cold. Remove cinnamon stick before serving.

Yield: 5 cups.

Peach or Apple Chutney
"traditional accompaniment to curry dishes"

½ pound onions, chopped	2 teaspoons mustard seed
½ pound raisins	2 teaspoons chili powder
2 cloves garlic, chopped	Pinch of cayenne pepper
4 pounds peeled peaches or apples, sliced	2 tablespoons salt
	1½ pounds brown sugar
1 cup preserved ginger	2 cups vinegar

Cook all ingredients slowly 4½ hours until thick and brown. Seal hot chutney in hot sterilized jars.

For a different and easy hors d'oeuvre, spoon some chutney over rectangles of cream cheese and allow to reach room temperature.

Yield: 2 quarts.

Green Tomato Mincemeat
"use up green tomatoes at the end of the season"

1 peck (8 quarts) green tomatoes, finely chopped	5 pounds sugar
	1 tablespoon salt
4 quarts peeled, chopped apples	2 tablespoons cinnamon
4 pounds raisins	1 tablespoon ground cloves
1 cup lemon juice	1 tablespoon nutmeg

In a large kettle, bring tomatoes and 1 quart water to a boil; rinse tomatoes in cold water and drain. Repeat this process two more times, adding 1 quart of water each time.

Add apples, raisins, lemon juice, sugar and salt. Bring to boil; lower heat and simmer several hours until thick. Add spices, mixing well.

Seal hot mincemeat in hot sterilized quart jars.

See note under Traditional Mincemeat for possible uses.

Yield: 6 quarts.

Variation: 2 pounds currants can be substituted for 2 pounds raisins.

Traditional Mincemeat

"Discover why mincemeat pie is one of America's great traditional holiday desserts."

1½-2 pounds beef roast
(chuck, pot, etc.)
Salt and pepper
½ cup suet
5 cups apples, finely diced
1 pound raisins
1 cup currants
⅓ cup diced candied orange and
lemon peel combined
1 cup packed brown sugar

¼ cup molasses
1 tablespoon cinnamon
½ teaspoon salt
½ teaspoon nutmeg
½ teaspoon ground cloves
½ teaspoon allspice
½ teaspoon mace
¼ teaspoon pepper
3 cups cider
Grated peel of 2 lemons

Simmer meat in water in covered pan until tender. Salt and pepper to taste. (Broth can be used for soup.) Finely dice meat (about 2 cups are needed) and suet, or put through food grinder using medium blade.

In heavy Dutch oven, mix together all ingredients. Cook over very low heat, stirring frequently until thick and well blended, about 2 hours. Watch carefully to avoid burning.

Mincemeat will keep for a week refrigerated or can be frozen. Use in pies, cookies, stuffed apples, apple crisp and many other creative ways. If desired, 2 tablespoons brandy may be added for each pie.

Yield: enough for three or four 9-inch pies.

Herb Blend for Meats and Vegetables

"salt-free need not mean bland"

1 teaspoon dried basil
1 teaspoon dried marjoram
1 teaspoon dried thyme
1 teaspoon dried oregano
1 teaspoon dried parsley
1 teaspoon dried savory

1 teaspoon ground cloves
1 teaspoon ground mace
1 teaspoon black pepper
¼ teaspoon ground nutmeg
¼ teaspoon cayenne

Combine ingredients and store in air-tight jar.

Yield: 3½ tablespoons.

Spice Shaker
"a zippy alternative to salt"

1 tablespoon dry mustard	1 teaspoon garlic powder
1 tablespoon onion powder	½ teaspoon white pepper
1 tablespoon paprika	¼ teaspoon dried basil

Combine ingredients and store in air-tight jar.

Yield: about ¼ cup.

Make your own herb vinegars

Seasoning with herb vinegar is an endless adventure to add interest and new taste sensations. Try one in your favorite salad dressing or in a marinade. There are many uses for herb vinegars . . . as many as you want to experiment with. Herbed vinegars are simple to make from ordinary supermarket vinegars — white, red, cider, or wine — and dried or fresh herbs. The basic recipe is simple.

1 quart vinegar
4 teaspoons of dried herbs
   OR 2 cups of fresh

Bring vinegar to a boil, turn off heat. Put herbs in large clean jar. Pour slightly cooled vinegar over herbs, seal and store in dark room for a week — stirring a few times — strain, and pour into colored bottles. With your own handmade labels, herbed vinegars make original gifts.

Basil or sweet basil: especially flavorful on tomatoes and leafy greens; use as marinade for fish, meats, poultry, or game; use in ragouts, sauces, and salad dressings, in egg dishes, soups.

Basil or purple basil: same as sweet basil vinegar; gives the vinegar a rich burgundy color and makes an impressive gift.

Chives: use in marinade for roasts and in dressings where chive flavor is desired.

Dill: use in salad dressings; to marinate vegetables; in potato salad; and as baste for fish and poultry.

Garlic: use in marinade for meat, roasts, poultry, game; in salad dressings, sauces, soups and in any food in which garlic flavor is desired.

Mint: use in marinade for lamb and roast meats; also in salad dressings.

Salad burnet: lends a cucumber flavor to the vinegar; when used in salad dressing it gives the cucumber taste without the digestive problems sometimes caused by the cucumber.

Shallot: use the same as chives or garlic vinegar.

Tarragon: use in marinades for fish, meats, roasts, poultry; use in sauces (white sauce, Bearnaise, tartar sauce), soups and favorite French dressing.

Thyme: use in marinades for meat, fish; use in stews, chowders, salad dressing, fish and shellfish sauce.

Herb blends: suggested herb blends for vinegars: parsley, marjoram, thyme / basil, oregano, parsley / summer savory, basil, parsley / garlic, rosemary, thyme. Use in marinades for meats, roasts, game; in salad dressings or meat sauces.

Tips on herbs

☐ Herbs are to enhance, not to overpower the flavor of food. Use a delicate touch in cooked dishes such as stews, soups, roasts and casseroles. Experiment by adding a little more to taste to develop your preference.

☐ Fresh herbs are more flavorful and can be used in greater quantity than dried ones. A good rule of thumb is to use about three times as much fresh herbs for dry.

☐ It is better to use a small amount of an herb to begin with. You can always add more to taste.

☐ With a hot food, it is better to add herbs toward the end of cooking. In seasoning cold foods, do just the opposite. Add the herbs at the beginning. The longer they are combined, the more the flavor develops.

☐ Be creative and experiment and mix your own herbs. Get to know which herbs you prefer and in what combination.

☐ Herbs are a fine substitute for salt for those people cutting down or on a low sodium diet.

☐ Keep your herb shelf stocked and away from too much light and heat. Never keep herbs over the stove.

☐ Use herbs to your own taste. Don't just add to foods just to add to foods.

CONTRIBUTORS

Contributions for THE PEOPLE'S CHOICE COOKBOOK were solicited and received from the dedicated membership and loyal friends of LWVMN. Many more good recipes were submitted than could be included. All were edited for accuracy and clarity; some were modified to reflect current health trends. Diligence and hard work characterized the members' involvement, from the cookbook committee to the fifty-six testers who cooked, served and tasted each recipe. Their work enhances the value of this book and we applaud them.

It is with special thanks that we salute these people . . .

Ginny Allen	Edna Broten	Betty Dunlap	✔Nancy Grimsby
✔Mary Adair	Muriel Humphrey Brown	David Durenberger	Joan Growe
Aileen Albrecht	Carol Brozic	Penny Durenberger	Rosemary Guttormson
Lee Alexander	Philip Brunelle		
Rosalie Allard	Audrey Brunning	Elizabeth Ebbott	Georgeann Hall
Douglas Amdahl	✔Joann Buie	Sandy Eliason	Judy Halley
Phyllis Ammentorp	Louis A. Buie, Jr.	Connie Ellis	George E. Harding
Celia Andersen	Eleanor Burdick	Faye Ellison	Helen M. Hart
Judy Andersen	✔Patricia Buysman	Mary Elrod	Mary Hartwig
Karen Anderson	Don Byerly	Linda Erickson	Patricia Hasselmo
Sharon Anderson	Byerly's	Elsie Evans	Mrs. Martin Hauser
✔Grace Andrews		Sally Evert	✔Hazel Helgeson
Bea Arett	Connie Cameron		Ellen Henden
✔Sherry Arndt	✔Prudence Cameron	Fairview-Southdale Hospital	Barbara Hendershott
Mary Ayde	Nancy Campbell	Anne B. Fenton	Carolyn Hendrixson
	Janet Cardle	Eleanor S. Fenton	✔Mary Hepokoski
Kay Bach	Nancy Carlson	✔Mimi Fetzler	✔Mary Hicken
Carol Bailey	Anne Carrier	Evelyn M. Fett	Donna Hipps
Dorie Barman	✔Cindy Chamberlin	Lorraine Fischer	✔Marilyn Hoeft
✔Diana Barsness	Pinky Charon	Lisa Fish, M.D.	Gladys Holst
Betty Bayless	✔Shirley Chenoweth	Marcia Fluer	Connie Hondl
Bemidji Area LWV	Ray Christensen	Renee Fordyce	Judy Hove
Favorite Wild Rice	✔Diane Christopher	Mary Forsythe	Helen Hunter
Recipes of Minnesota's	✔Judy Cipolla	Anne Francis	Lorraine Husnick
North Country	Helaine Cohen	Billie Franey	Paulette Hutton
Betty Benjamin	Jeanne Crampton	Jenny Froyd	
Barbara Benson	✔Laurie Culbert		Jean Ingham
Sally-Anne Benson	Jean Currie	Alice Gaede	Nancy Irsfeld
Rita Berens		Katherine Gallagher	✔Rose Isenhart
Linda Bergen	✔Dawn Darner	Cathy Gerster	
Julie Bjorkland	✔Maggie Davern	Beth Gillham	Carol Jackson
Virginia Bodine	Dorothy Davies	✔Linda Goese	✔Sara Jaehne
Rudy Boschwitz	Karen Dee	Doris Gordon	Charlotte Jenkins
Anthony Bouza	Zeta DeMarais	Ethel Goven	Jerry's
Dolores Bowman	Harriet Dieterich	✔Zelma Gray	Arlene Joern
Marsha Brandt	Claire Downes	Jean Greener	Betty Johnson
Jan Bray	Dave Duff	Diane Greensweig	Gustave F. Johnson
		Mindy Greiling	Marlene Johnson

✔ Tester

Phyllis Kahn
Muriel Keil
Glenn E. Kelley
Peggy Kelly
Polly Keppel
Mickey Kieffer
Sue Kirsch
Patricia Kratky
Rose Krauser
Marlene Krona

Dorothy Lace
Rose Lano
Robin Larkin
Susan LaRock
Diane Larson
Nikki Laub
Bernice Law
Olive S. Leikvold
Peggy Leppik
Jennifer Leslie
Virginia Levy
Sue Lewis
Mary Lindstrom
Bea Lipove
Pat Llona
Jeannette Lofstrom
Josephine Longpre
Naomi Loper
Dorothy Lucas
Pat Lucas
Peggy Lucas
Pat Lund
Lunds
Jack Lynch
Winifred Lyon

C. Peter Magrath
James H. Manahan
Julie Manfred
Mary Lou Manley
Mary Mantis
Laurel March
Anne M. Markfort
Carol Marshall

Louise Matthies
Pam Mattson
Clarice McCue
Kay McCulley
Cindy McGurk
Betty Ann McKaig
Hope Melton
Jessie Merrell
Connie Metcalf
Lillian Meyer
Ruth Ann Michnay
Martha Micks
Shirley Miedtke
Pat Miles
Jeanette Miller
Muriel A. Miller
Sandi Monahan
Joan Mondale
Walter Mondale
Dave Moore
Jean Moore
Nadeen Mutsch

Alice Neidigh
Catherine Nelson
Geri Nelson
Jeanne Nelson
Lin Neu
Irene Nordling
Judy Nordlund

Betty Obenchain
Mary Ojeda
Pearl Okubo
LaNelle Olsen
Martha Oye

Fern Panda
Irene Parsons
Mrs. Curtis Paulsen
Diane Peil
Lola Perpich
Rudy Perpich
C. Donald Peterson
Gretchen Peterson
Juanita Peterson

Peterson, Tews, and
    Squires Law Firm
Iva Platt
Merdith Poland
Mary Pooley
Joan Popowich
Patricia Priesmeyer
Ann Pugliese

Gretchen Quie

Dorothy Rakow
Jim Ramstad
Lois G. Raps
Marilyn Rehnberg
Leola Rempel
Carmen Rey
Florence Richardson
Shirley Rickord
Betty Ripke
Sara Russell (Betty Crocker
    Marketing Division)
Denise Rydholm

Flora Sage
Betty Sailer
Jane Salada
Faye Sargent
Duffy Sauer
Sally Sawyer
Emily Schmitz
George M. Scott
Joyce H. Scott
Donna Scudder
Joyce Secrist
Suzanne Sedgewick
Marree Seitz
Lexi Selvig
Sandra Shanley
SHAPE
Hazel Shimmin
Elizabeth Skeba
Marie Skinner
Pam Sohlberg
Marcia Spagnola
Ginny Stabnow

Jacqueline Stalley
Jane Stein
Ella Stene
Marilee Stevens
Kay Stiegler
Sally Stoppel
Virginia Sweeny

Jean Tews
Genevieve Thayer
Ann Thomas
Kay Thompson
Peggy Thompson
Rosemary Thorsen
Mimi Titzler
John J. Todd
Ann Tulloch

Bettyann Ungemach
Rose Mary Utne

Doris Van Campen
Kathleen Vellenga
Betsy Vinz

Helen Waldron
Zilla Way
Sandy Weber
Donna Wegley
Marty Wells
Leah Wenker
Donna Wert
Lynne Westphal
Donna Wiedenman
Carole Wiederhorn
Barbara Wilkinson
Isabelle Wille
Rita Wilson
Molly Woehrlin
Dora Woyda
Gloria Wynnemer

Mildred Zeigler
Marva Zima
Ginny Zimmer

INDEX

The League of Women Voters of Minnesota . . .

(LWVMN) is an active and vital community resource and has been since 1919. The primary purpose of LWVMN is to promote political responsibility through informed and active participation of citizens in government.

Our accomplishments in voter service and citizen information are possible only because of the vast network of volunteers throughout the state. The 3,400 members in 65 local Leagues make the decisions for the League, choosing the issues on which to concentrate study and action efforts, and deciding how best to provide their local communities with election information. Many members also volunteer to carry out the state and regional projects of the LWVMN.

Membership in the League is open to women and men who are 18 and over. A person may join the local, state or national level of LWV and is part of the whole organization, with the opportunity to study issues of international, state or local concern. Members help with projects that run the gamut from registering voters at a local shopping center to publishing a book on Minnesota's Native American population to producing a televised presidential debate. LWV's successes and accomplishments are shared by the individual volunteers who make things happen.

The League is a nonpartisan organization and does not support or oppose any political party or candidate. We have earned our reputation for unbiased, objective publications and public forums.

For more information about the LWV in your community, write or call:

The League of Women Voters of Minnesota
555 Wabasha, St. Paul, MN 55102
(612) 224-5445

Jean Tews
President, League of Women Voters of Minnesota

The LWVMN is truly a grassroots organization, with 65 local Leagues active throughout Minnesota in these communities:

Alexandria	Excelsior/Deephaven Area	Morrrison County	St. Paul
Anoka/Blaine/Coon Rapids	Freeborn County	Mounds View	St. Peter
Arden Hills/Shoreview	Fridley	New Brighton	Shakopee
Austin	Golden Valley	New Ulm	Stevens County
Battle Lake	Grand Rapids Area	Northern Dakota County	Wayzata Area
Bemidji Area	Grant County	Area	West Dakota County Area
Bloomington	Hibbing	Northfield	Westonka
Brooklyn Center	Houston County	Owatonna	White Bear Lake/North
Brooklyn Park	Hutchinson	Red Wing	Oaks
Buffalo/Monticello Area	Jackson Area	Richfield	Wilkin County
Cass Lake/Walker Area	Mahtomedi Area	Robbinsdale	Willmar
Columbia Heights	Mankato Area	Rochester	Winona
Crystal/New Hope	Marshall	Rock County	Woodbury/Cottage Grove
Detroit Lakes	Mid-Mesabi	Roseville	Worthington
Duluth	Minneapolis	St. Anthony	Council of Metropolitan
East Faribault County	Minnetonka/Eden Prairie/	St. Cloud Area	Area Leagues
Eastern Carver County	Hopkins Area	St. Croix Area	Hennepin County Leagues
Edina	Moorhead	St. Louis Park	of Women Voters

THE PEOPLE'S CHOICE COOKBOOK ✓

Make checks payable and send to: **COOKBOOK, LWVMN, 555 Wabasha, St. Paul, MN 55102.**
All proceeds will be used by the LWVMN to promote political responsibility through an informed citizenry.

Please send _____ cookbooks @ $8.95 _____
tax incl.
Postage and handling each book   1.50 _____

Send books to: TOTAL ENCLOSED _____

_____

_____
ADDRESS

_____
CITY   STATE   ZIP

☐ Check here if this is a gift order. Please enclose a gift card and mailing instructions.

THANK YOU FOR YOUR ORDER!

THE PEOPLE'S CHOICE COOKBOOK ✓

Make checks payable and send to: **COOKBOOK, LWVMN, 555 Wabasha, St. Paul, MN 55102.**
All proceeds will be used by the LWVMN to promote political responsibility through an informed citizenry.

Please send _____ cookbooks @ $8.95 _____
tax incl.
Postage and handling each book   1.50 _____

Send books to: TOTAL ENCLOSED _____

_____

_____
ADDRESS

_____
CITY   STATE   ZIP

☐ Check here if this is a gift order. Please enclose a gift card and mailing instructions.

THANK YOU FOR YOUR ORDER!

THE PEOPLE'S CHOICE COOKBOOK ✓

Make checks payable and send to: **COOKBOOK, LWVMN, 555 Wabasha, St. Paul, MN 55102.**
All proceeds will be used by the LWVMN to promote political responsibility through an informed citizenry.

Please send _____ cookbooks @ $8.95 _____
tax incl.
Postage and handling each book   1.50 _____

Send books to: TOTAL ENCLOSED _____

_____

_____
ADDRESS

_____
CITY   STATE   ZIP

☐ Check here if this is a gift order. Please enclose a gift card and mailing instructions.

THANK YOU FOR YOUR ORDER!